"on frequent journeys, in
dangers from rivers,
dangers from robbers,
dangers from my own race,
dangers from Gentiles,
dangers in the city,
dangers in the wilderness,
dangers among false brothers"

(2 Corinthians 11:26)

SAINT PAUL IN ANATOLIA
AND CYPRUS

Fatih Cimok

A TURİZM YAYINLARI

FRONT COVER
Mosaic of Paul from the Kariye Museum
(former church of the monastery of St Saviour in Chora). 1315-21. İstanbul.

BACK COVER
Map of the eastern Mediterranean, central Anatolia and Cyprus from *Tabula Peutingeriana* (Peutinger Map).
This map, which shows the road network of the Roman empire, is a twelfth-century copy of fourth-century original.
Some of the cities Paul visited during his journeys can be easily distinguished.

PICTURES
Archives of A Turizm Yayınları

First printing 1999
Third printing 2001

ISBN 975-7199-05-2

Copyright © A Turizm Yayınları

PUBLISHERS
A Turizm Yayınları Ltd Şti
Şifa Hamamı Sokak 18/2,
Sultanahmet, İstanbul 34400, Turkey
Tel: (0212) 516 24 97 Fax: (0212) 516 41 65
e-mail: aturizm @ superonline.com

Contents

Decoration on a door jamb after which the Roman monument near the Magnesian Gate of Ephesus was named the 'tomb of Luke,' the author of the Third Gospel and the Acts of the Apostles.

Introduction

Antioch on the Orontes and Ephesus, cities second in wealth and importance in the Roman empire only to Alexandria in Egypt and to Rome itself, were inseparably linked with the early history of Christianity. Indeed it was in Antioch that the word 'Christians' was used to refer to the adherents to the new religion. Yet it was not only in these great cities that the new religion found adherents, for it gathered them also in far distant towns and communities of Anatolia. From the Mediterranean coast, through the uplands of Galatia and to the well-settled valleys of the west, to all these places, on foot or by slow moving ships, Paul, the tireless apostle, carried the Christian message. At each place he gathered into fellowships of churches, men and women, rich and poor, who had accepted the message and he nurtured the faithful, both by his presence and his letters.

Although born as a movement within Judaism, it was in Anatolia that the new religion rapidly took root, largely as a result of Paul's missionary work in the mid-first century. It was mostly here that Christianity developed away from its origins in rural Palestine to become a religion of the urban Greco-Roman world.

Paul's missionary journeys through southern and western Anatolia are recorded in the second and longer part of the Acts of the Apostles, written in Greek by the evangelist Luke, author of the Third Gospel. A sequel to his Gospel, the Acts of the Apostles continues Luke's history of Christian origins and tells the story of the early church and how it spread from the Jews to the Gentiles, largely through the efforts of Paul.

Reused furniture leg from Philadelphia (Alaşehir). Late Roman period. Manisa Archaeological Museum. It is decorated with a menorah and an inscription which in Greek reads: 'Jewish memoriam (tomb)'. The menorah is flanked by *ethrog*, a citrus fruit (left) and *lulab*, a palm branch.

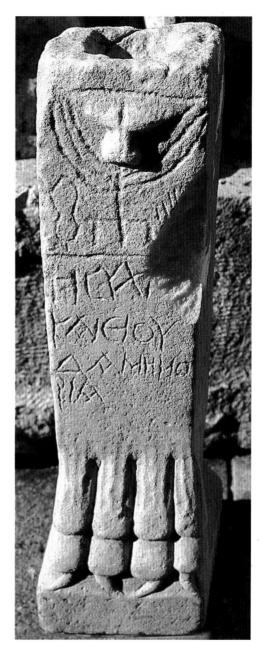

The works of various Greek and Roman authors and other contemporary sources, as well as the discoveries of archaeology, help to shed light on this period and on the world in which Paul travelled. However, it should be remembered that many of the Roman building remains at places he visited are of later date. At some sites there has been little or no excavation and in towns and cities that have been continuously inhabited there is sometimes virtually nothing to be seen, as the remains of earlier ages lie beneath existing structures.

Nevertheless, in one form or another, be it a stretch of Roman road, an inscribed pedestal whose statue may have ended up somewhere nobody knows, the remains of a pagan shrine, a bridge still in use after some two millennia or a dedication to Artemis, such evidence can help us to understand something of the Greco-Roman world of Anatolia in which Paul lived. Ultimately Anatolia became the most christianized region in the Roman empire and it was here, on the Bosphorus, at Byzantium, that Constantine the Great would found his new and Christian capital as New Rome and dedicate it in 330.

This book is intended primarily as a companion guide for Paul's journeys in Turkey and Cyprus and it does not, except in passing, consider the apostle's travels elsewhere. The same is true for his letters. Also, since the subject matter of the book is Paul's journeys, effort has been spent to keep the information, which is not directly related to these and to the first century, to a minimum. Thus, the reader should not expect to find the usual sightseeing information which is available in the other books about the cities Paul visited. Also, from his letters only the sections, which are directly related to Anatolian journeys, are included in the text.

Paul the apostle.
Detail from the
Dormition.
Nineteenth-century
icon. Sinop
Museum.

PAUL THE APOSTLE

Paul, the great Christian missionary, was born in the Cilician city of Tarsus perhaps a few years after Jesus was born in Bethlehem. His family was Jewish and from them he inherited Roman citizenship.

Paul was privileged to have been born a Roman citizen at a time when it was not yet a universal right for people in the empire.[1] Initially confined to freeborn natives of the city itself, as Roman control was extended throughout Italy and then to the lands bordering the Mediterranean and beyond, certain individuals and communities were given this right. At the time of Paul's ancestors, one way of attaining to Roman citizenship was serving in the Roman army for twenty-five years. However, because of Sabbath and Mosaic food prescriptions this profession would not have been normally possible for a Jew. The second way by which Roman citizenship could be gained was slavery. It was known that during the century preceding Paul's time, thousands of people were deported from the eastern Levant to Italy and made slaves. In the course of time some of these were able to distinguish themselves by their skill and profession and were either freed by their masters or bought their freedom and thus were given Roman citizenship. A remote ancestor of Paul, after obtaining this citizenship, seems to have returned to his native city Tarsus and reestablished the family business. Neither Acts nor his letters give enough information about Paul's ancestors or parents. He is known to have had a married sister in Jerusalem and a nephew (Acts 23:16). From one of his letters we learn that he had some distant relatives (Rom 16:7, 11, 21). Some scholars believe that his words 'If the unbeliever separates, however, let him separate' (1 Cor 7:15) refer to the fact that he was married and upon his return to Tarsus converted, his wife may have deserted him.

The most important privilege that Roman citizenship conferred on a subject was that he enjoyed legal protection and could not be scourged and had the right of appeal to the emperor in person, hence Paul's journey to Rome to appeal to Caesar. It is thought that during the floggings he endured (2 Cor 11:25), the apostle may have not revealed his citizenship because of the fact that he wished to follow Christ in his suffering. Even if they were condemned to death, Roman citizens could not be crucified. In the course of time, however, it seems that the avaricious government officials began selling this right as

"Are they Hebrews? So am I. Are they Israelites? So am I. Are they descendants of Abraham? So am I" (2 Cor 11:22).

[1] At that time, a right perhaps about one out of ten people, altogether about five million, possessed in the whole Roman empire.

admitted by the cohort commander Claudius Lysias to Paul: 'I acquired this citizenship for a large sum of money' (Acts 22:28). A citizen's responsibilities included the performance of military service, from which Jews were exempted on religious grounds such as Sabbath and kosher food.

There are several theories about why the apostle chose the name by which he is known today. Paul's *cognomen*, 'Paulus' the name by which he was known, was probably chosen because of its similarity to his Hebrew name 'Saul'; as it means 'small' it might also have been an allusion to his size. New citizens would take on the first two names, the *praenomen* and *nomen*, of the official granting their admission. Thus, 'Paul' might have also been the name of the patron of that unknown ancestor who granted the latter Roman citizenship. By the time of the early empire, when Paul was born, the use of two names seems to have been acceptable, at any rate in the New Testament, thus Judas called Barsabbas (Acts 15:22) etc. The apostle must have had a second name which is not mentioned. Whatever the reason for choosing it, 'Paul' was a rare name even among Gentiles. It has also been suggested that the apostle may have chosen the name after his first Gentile convert known by name, Sergius Paulus in Cyprus.

Paul would probably have carried a birth registration certificate for identification purposes when travelling. The information of citizenship was included in the birth registers whose authorized copy could be obtained to be displayed when questioned by authorities. From the various references to his Roman citizenship in Acts, it is clear that Paul valued this privilege which certainly helped him at times of trouble.

Acts and his letters make it clear that Paul worked to support himself and those who were with him. This was a period when boys usually learnt their craft from their fathers, which was often the family's business. The nature of his work is clearly stated as tentmaking when he stayed with Aquila and Priscilla: 'and, because he practiced the same trade, stayed with them and worked; for they were tentmakers by trade' (Acts 18:3).

Given Paul's rabbinical background there is nothing extraordinary about this; Jewish sources indicate that rabbis were expected to work and not to profit from their study and interpretation of the Torah. This does appear to have been the case and there are several references to working hands. In his address to the elders of Ephesus the apostle reminds them of this, saying 'these very hands have served my needs' (Acts 20:34); also when he says 'we toil, working with our hands' (1 Cor 4:12) or 'nor did we eat food received free from anyone.

"On the contrary, in toil and drudgery, night and day we worked, so as not to burden any of you" (2 Thes 3:8).

Nomads in tents of black goat-hair cloth, or *cilicium* in Smooth Cilicia (Cilicia Pedias).

On the contrary, in toil and drudgery, night and day we worked, so as not to burden any of you' (2 Thes 3:8). These remarks also answer the questions about financial sources of the apostle's missionary journeys. In spite of the gifts he seems to have received from Christian communities for which he expresses his gratitude, most of the time he relied on his own resources, a fact which is often hinted at in his letters and clearly expressed in the one addressed to the Philippians: 'I find myself, to be self-sufficient...Still, it was kind of you to share in my distress' (Phil 4:11,14); 'For even when I was at Thessalonica you sent me something for my needs' (Phil 4:16).

It is possible that Paul's family had made their money equipping the Roman legionaries, who used very large tents, made of leather panels stretched together so that rain water would run off. The Roman legions stationed in Syria may not have required leather tents but used the traditional goat-hair tents similar to those of the present day nomads. These are made of the rough cloth manufactured from goat's hair, which in the past was known as *cilicium*,[2] and took its name from Cilicia. Tentmaking might well have embraced not only the manufacture and the repair of these large, military tents, but also a range of related leather and woven goods. Apart from military tents, there would have been considerable demand for awnings, booths and canopies from vendors at market places and elsewhere. Since there were many Roman legions based on the upper Euphrates and in Syria tentmaking was perhaps a very profitable profession, considering the flourishing animal husbandry in the region since early antiquity.

Within the family and Jewish community he was called Saul, Paul being the Latinized form he used when speaking Greek; this he did well and idiomatically, as befitted one who had grown up in a cosmopolitan and largely Greek city. He would probably also have spoken Aramaic, the language of Palestine and the whole Near East, where he spent fairly extended periods. As he had a strict Jewish upbringing, which was followed by study in Jerusalem where he trained to be a rabbi,[3] he would have known Hebrew too. In the Jewish Diaspora he dwelled on his Jewish background. Elsewhere, in conversing with Greeks he spoke their native tongue and in the world of Romans he would emphasize his Roman citizenship.

[2] Turkish 'çul'.

[3] In Hebrew 'my master' or 'my teacher'. The title was conferred on a man by the Sanhedrin.

If Paul's family were not members of the Pharisees, then at some stage he became one; this was a sect that observed strict ritual purity and adherence to Mosaic law. Its members thought that they alone could interpret the Torah correctly and felt their responsibility to teach other Jews the ways of living righteously. Saul, the name chosen for him, was the name of the first king of the Jews about a millennium before. The Pharisees and other such Jewish sects regarded the Christian movement as a threat and so it is as a persecutor of the Christians and witness to the death of Stephen, the first Christian martyr, that Paul first appears in Acts.

The only available physical information about the apostle comes from the apocryphal Acts of Paul. Here, Onesiphorus, a man of Iconium, who wants to receive Paul in his house, waits on the 'king's highway' coming from Lystra, for 'a man of little stature, thin-haired upon the head, crooked in the legs, of good state of body, with eyebrows joining, and nose somewhat hooked, full of grace: for sometimes he appeared like a man, and sometimes he had the face of an angel', his description by Titus whom Paul had sent before him to the city to announce his arrival. The fact that the commander of the soldiers who arrested Paul in Jerusalem thought that his prisoner may have been 'the Egyptian' they were looking for (Acts 21:38), may imply that the apostle had a wheat-coloured complexion. The apostle himself may have been conscious of his insignificant physical look because he admits that this could be used against him by his enemies (2 Cor 10:10). The 'short dark hair, domed brow and black, pointed beard' became the distinct features of his physiognomy in Byzantine art.

Paul is not included among the Twelve Apostles, but regarded as the thirteenth apostle. By the sixth century he replaced Matthias, who had taken the place of the traitor Judas Iscariot after the latter's death (Acts 1:26). Byzantine iconography usually depicted the apostle looking to his right, with the book of his letters in his left hand, his other hand is in a gesture of address, garbed in a dark green or dark blue tunic on which he wears an open dark red cloak.

As is well-known, Paul was converted to Christianity after a vision of the risen Christ appeared to him on the road to Damascus. Blinded, he was led to Damascus and there, after three days of fasting and praying, he recovered his sight, was filled with the Holy Spirit and then baptized (Acts 9:3-19; 22:6-16; 26:12-18).

There have been innumerable attempts by theologians and others to understand and explain precisely what happened at this turning point in his

"Circumcised on the eighth day, of the race of Israel, of the tribe of Benjamin, a Hebrew of Hebrew parentage, in observance of the law a Pharisee" (Phil 3:5).

life. All that can be said briefly, is that Paul's theology should perhaps be traced to his experience of conversion. He claimed to have received his gospel 'through a revelation of Jesus Christ' (Gal 1:12); this in turn led to his proclamation of salvation through the reconciling grace of God; thus the death of Christ for the atonement of sins was God reconciling the world to himself through Christ.

In whichever way Paul's vision and conversion are understood, it is clear, that like the prophets of the Old Testament, he saw himself as chosen by God for a specific task, namely, to be an apostle[4] (messenger of the church) to Gentiles. For him the Christian message, that Christ died to atone for the sins of man and for the salvation of man, was resurrected and ascended to heaven, was both the fulfilment of Jewish messianic hopes and the basis for a united humanity; love, reconciliation and salvation were central themes of his theology. This clear message of the apostle may have been the reason why he did not became an object of a separate Christian cult, such as that of John in Ephesus, Barnabas in Cyprus or Peter in Antioch.

After his conversion, there followed a period of solitude in Arabia (Gal 1:17), a word which is probably to be understood as somewhere in Syria, before he returned to Damascus where he spent three years preaching the doctrine of the crucified and risen Christ. This antagonized the Jews of Damascus. 'But his disciples took him one night and let him down through an opening in the wall, lowering him in a basket' (Acts 9:25). He returned to Jerusalem and began preaching the name of the Lord. Subsequently, when the Jews 'tried to kill him' he was sent to his native city of Tarsus.

He was subsequently fetched and brought to Antioch on the Orontes by Barnabas to help him there. At Antioch, the converts included many Gentiles, a situation which ultimately led to a crisis from which Paul emerged as the advocate of Gentile conversion. The controversy, which lasted several years, had at its heart Jewish purity laws, which made Jews reluctant to eat with non-Jews. The latter, not being circumcised or bound by the obligations of Mosaic dietary observances, were regarded as impure. As the breaking of bread and the drinking of wine were central to Christian fellowship, there was clearly an impasse. The resolution of this, Paul's decision to convert Gentiles, ensured that Christianity did not remain just another Jewish sect, but in time became a universal religion.

(opposite) Detail from a mosaic where Paul is shown being lowered in a basket over the walls of Damascus. Late twelfth century. Cathedral of Montreale. Palermo.

[4] Greek *apostolos*, 'emissary'.

PAVLVS · P̄ FENESTRAM · IN SPORTA · DIMISSVS
PER · MVRV̄ · EFFVGIT · MAN DAMASCENO · R̄

S · PAVL̄

From Antioch on the Orontes, in about 45, Paul and Barnabas set out on their first main missionary journey to Cyprus and then to Pisidia and southern Galatia in central Anatolia, returning to Antioch on the Orontes after two, perhaps three years by sea from the Pamphylian city of Attaleia by way of Palestine.

On a second journey, about 49-52 accompanied by Silas — and Timothy after Lystra — Paul travelled through Cilicia to Galatia, then to Alexandria Troas and on to Greece, once again returning by sea to Caesarea and from there to Antioch on the Orontes, this time by way of Ephesus.

On his third missionary journey, about 53-58, Paul again visited the Galatian cities on his way to Ephesus, where he remained for about three years. From there he visited Greece to which he returned again, by way of Alexandria Troas, on finally leaving from Miletus.

His last brief visit to his native land was whilst being taken as a captive to Rome, when ships were changed at Andriace, port of Myra in Lycia. The date of most of Paul's journeys corresponds to the reign of the emperor Claudius (41-54) whose rule was known to be milder and more peaceful than that of his predecessor Gaius Caligula (37-41) and his successor Nero (54-68). When the latter succeeded Claudius in 54, Paul was on his third journey. It is not known if he would have been able to carry out his journeys during the persecutions of Caligula or Nero.

After his third missionary journey, Paul went to Jerusalem. There he caused a riot by the Jews, who thought, mistakenly, that he had broken Jewish law by taking a Gentile into the sacred ground of the Temple. He was arrested, but as a Roman citizen, was treated fairly. Paul was then taken to Caesarea, where the Roman governor kept him in prison to avoid problems with the Sanhedrin.[5] When the next governor tried to send him to the Sanhedrin for trial, Paul claimed his right as a Roman citizen to be put on trial at Rome. He arrived there about 61 and lived under house arrest for two years. The unfinished narrative of Acts closes with him awaiting trial.

The circumstances of Paul's death are not known and there is conflicting evidence. According to one tradition he made a further missionary journey before being rearrested, imprisoned in Rome and sentenced to death. The most widely accepted view is that he was killed in about 62-67 during the persecution of Christians in Nero's reign as told in the apocryphal Acts of Paul.

[5] Jewish supreme council and court of justice during the period.

One of the two pieces of identical stones which survived from the destruction of the Jerusalem Temple by Titus in 70 CE. İstanbul Archaeological Museums. The inscription in Greek reads: 'No intruder is allowed in the courtyard and within the wall surrounding the temple. Those who enter will invite death for themselves'. The second inscription is fragmentary and in the Rockefeller Museum in Jerusalem. Paul was seen in Jerusalem in the company of a Greek called Trophimus the Ephesian, and assumed that he had contradicted God's law by taking him into the Temple. This was most unlikely, for Paul knew as well as anyone that no Gentile might pass the barrier.

Obverse of a bronze *sestertius*, sesterce of Claudius (41-54) who was the Roman emperor at the time of Paul's journeys. Diametre 30/31 mm. Weight 27,99 gr. İstanbul Archaeological Museums.

A section of the Roman mountain road which climbed the Taurus chain north of Antalya, and connected Perge to western Anatolia. It is paved with unhewn stones and for the borders larger stones have been used.

TRAVEL AND TRANSPORT IN PAUL'S TIME

Over a period of some ten years in the middle of the first century, Paul made three missionary journeys, travelling through Anatolia and Greece spreading the gospel. In the course of these, he visited much of Anatolia, probably walking a good deal of the way, accompanied by one or more companions.

It has been estimated that Paul travelled some 20,000 km on his missionary journeys, even if a fourth journey did not take place. A considerable part of this was overland through Anatolia, on Roman roads which followed the ancient routes that trailed the natural river and mountain passes which had been used for military transportation since antiquity. The Romans had began to construct these roads immediately after they established the province of Asia (western Anatolia) in the 130s BCE and by the time of Paul had extended their network covering southern Anatolia as far as Syria proper. A part of this ancient military net which ran through Pisidia and southern Galatia during the Roman period was known as the Via Sebaste. Paul and his companions were able to make their missionary journeys with relative ease and safety largely because of the Roman presence. Under the *Pax Romana*, the Roman peace instituted 'by Augustus, the roads were by and large kept free of brigands and in good repair'.

These roads were carefully engineered and built to carry the Roman armies, which at this date mostly consisted of troops and imperial officials, along the straightest route as swiftly as possible. The size and type of construction varied according to expected traffic, terrain and materials available, but the general principles of Roman road building were those described by the Greek author Plutarch, born about a decade before Paul's death: 'The roads were carried straight across the countryside. They were paved with hewn stones and bolstered underneath with masses of tight packed gravel; hollows were filled in, and torrents or ravines that cut across the route were bridged.'

The milestones[1] placed along the road usually showed the distance in Roman miles[2] but sometimes carried more detailed information, such as the name of

[1] The logic of a Roman milestone is contrary to that of a modern road-sign, so that it does not read 'Ephesus 10 miles', but 'From Ephesus 10 miles'.

[2] Latin *mille*, 1.48 km.

Roman milestone at Pozantı (near ancient Podandos), some 25 km north of the Cilician Gates. After giving the titles of the emperor Caracalla in Latin the inscription reads: 'repaired the Via Tauri which was dilapidated with age, by levelling mountains, smashing rocks, widening carriageways and building bridges. From the Gates 15 miles'. The last sentence is repeated in Greek. 217 CE.

the person who built or repaired the road, the number of available cisterns or garrisons or regulations of transportation. A bilingual edict — in Latin and in Greek[3] — and dating from the period Paul was born, fixes the number of animals that the people of Sagalassus (Ağlasun) were obliged to provide for different types of officials and the cost of such services, and the priority of the various kinds of officials and officers who might require them and thus it shows how much the Roman governor of the time cared for orderly transportation in his region.

At the time Paul travelled on these roads the regular posting stages belonging to the Roman government post were not yet known. The information about the inns of the period is not flattering. They were known to be dirty and dangerous spots. In the apocryphal Acts of John, the apostle, as he travelled from Ephesus to Laodicea (on the Lycus river), when bothered by bed bugs in the inn where he spent the night, banished them from his room. Nevertheless, next morning he found the insects waiting outside for his permission to return to their dwelling.

Ancient literature gives the impression that people preferred, when or where this was possible, to stay at other people's houses. If they had no acquaintances, arriving in an unknown town, they probably walked to the shrine of their cult, in the case of Jews to the synagogue, or to the market place with the members of their profession or guild, and introducing themselves expected an offer of hospitality. Being of the same country, religion or profession may have increased one's chance of receiving an invitation. At the time of Paul's journeys some of the synagogues in Anatolia and Greece probably had hostels. If one, however, remembers what the apostle preached and how the Jewish communities reacted, Paul should not have expected much hospitality from his own race. Acts mentions Paul's overnights at friends' houses such as at Lydia's in Philippi (Acts 16:15) and the tentmakers Aquila and Priscilla's in Corinth (Acts 18:3), Mnason's in Jerusalem (Acts 21:16),

[3] Burdur Archaeological Museum.

and others. This is also expressed by Paul himself when he wrote to Philemon of Colossae and asked him to prepare a guest room for him (Phlm 22). Acts shows that the apostle did not like travelling alone. One of the reasons for this may have been his sickness to which he is thought to have referred as 'a thorn in the flesh' or 'a messanger of Satan'. On the other hand Jesus also says that his disciples would travel in companion with another brother.

The period of Paul's travels in Anatolia saw a considerable expansion of prosperity and the roads were increasingly used by traders and private travellers. The worn out pavements on the busy main highways indicate a traffic of pack animals, mainly donkeys or mules and farm wagons with heavy loads drawn by teams of oxen as well as an assortment of carts and carriages. Few people other than the cavalry rode horses; it was tiring and uncomfortable, as stirrups had not yet been invented and saddles were fairly rudimentary; some however rode on mules. People travelled for many purposes: sightseeing, pilgrimage, health or business. Although seventy-two voyages of the merchant Titus Flavius Zeuxis of Hierapolis (Pamukkale) to Italy (p 24) may have been a rare experience it was not suprising to come across with people like the woman Lydia, from Thyateira (Akhisar) in Anatolia selling 'purple cloth' at Philippi across the Aegean (Acts 16:14) or Aquila and Priscilla, tentmakers originally from Pontus on the Black Sea, who had moved to Rome and then migrated to Corinth (Acts 18:2-3) and were about to move to Ephesus (Acts 18, 19).

Although there were many traders' vehicles or carriages bearing the wealthy to their estates, most travellers would have walked. Paul probably covered some 20 to 30 km a day on foot, sleeping at inns or the homes of friends or in the open when the weather was good along the way. He would have worn heavy shoes or sandals and perhaps a broad brimmed hat or a cloak with a hood and kept his money in a leather purse either on his belt or on a cord hung from the neck and a long staff to help him on rocky paths and against dogs. His provisions would have been probably loaded on a pack animal or carried by his companions.

Whilst most of Paul's missions were accomplished by walking, he travelled also by boat. Although considerably faster than land travel, it was also more dangerous, not just because of pirates who — despite some flattering claims

Relief with a coach from Thyateira. Late Roman period. Manisa Archaeological Museum. The vehicle has four six-spoked wheels and is drawn by a pair of

harnessed horses. The fragmentary inscription in Greek mentions a 'coach', 'Smaragdos' and a 'daughter', who are represented seated in litters behind the driver.

that they were cleared from the Mediterranean by the Romans — still roamed in some waters, but also because of the weather. Even in summer, voyages across the open sea were unpredictable. This was an era when passenger ships were not known. One had to go to the port and ask for a merchant vessel scheduled to sail to one's destination. Writing some three hundred years after the time of the apostle, Libanius, the pagan Antiochene orator remarks, 'In Constantinople I went down to the Great harbour and made the rounds asking about vessels sailing for Athens.' Having found a vessel that could take him to his destination, the passenger would have to wait near the harbour, perhaps several days, as perhaps the apostles had to do in Seleucia Pieria at the beginning of their first journey to sail to Cyprus and on many other occasions, for the right winds and omens. The apocyrphal Acts of Philip also informs us that at the port of Caesarea the apostle found a vessel bound for Carthage which had been waiting 'for twenty days' for the right winds.

By the first century the captains and pilots who navigated in the Mediterranean possessed information accumulated over the centuries since the Phoenicians. Although in the Mediterranean the winds and currents are known not to have changed for the last two thousand years, in order to minimize the dangers of sailing in the open sea, during this period, captains sailed without losing the sight of the coastline, a practice which lasted as late as the sixteenth century. The Mediterranean was good for sailing in the open sea except in winter when storms and fog affected visibility of the coast and stars. In fine weather captains either followed the Pole star or any landmark. With a few exceptions, it was always possible to see the silhouette of a mountain such as the peaks of the Taurus range of Anatolia, the African coastline or the islands. The sailing season was short and limited to the period of good weather, beginning in the early spring and lasting until late fall. Writing in the seventh century BCE, the Greek poet Hesiod limits the navigable season in the Mediterranean to the period between 5 May and 25 October. It may be for this reason that Paul cut his stay short when he stopped at Ephesus during his return from Corinth to Jerusalem at the end of his second journey (Acts 18:20). In winter when the skies were cloudy, the stars and sun, by which sailors found their course, were often not visible. The dangers of winter weather and tempests are vividly described in the account of the voyage that ended in shipwreck off Malta, when Paul was

...ΟΣ...
...ΥΙΟΣ ΖΕΥΣ ΕΡΓΑΣΤΗΣ
...ΥΣΑ ΣΥΠΕΡ ΜΑΛΕΟΝ ΕΙΣ
...ΙΑΝ ΠΙΟ ΑΣ ΕΒΔΟΜΗΚΟΝΤΑ
...ΟΡΑΤΕΣ ΚΕΥΑΣΕΝ ΤΟ ΜΝΗΜΕ...
...Ν ΕΑΥΤΟΙΣ ΚΑΙ ΤΟΙΣ ΤΕΚΝΟΙΣ ΦΛΑ...
...ΙΩ ΘΕΟΔΩΡΟ ΚΑΙ ΦΛΑ ΥΙΟ...
...ΟΥΔΑ ΚΑΙ Ω ΑΝ ΕΚΕΙΝΟΙ...
...ΚΥΝΧΩΡΗΣΩΣΙΝ

(opposite) Epitaph above the door of a tomb in the necropolis at Hierapolis. End of the first century CE. In Greek it reads: 'Titus Flavius Zeuxis, merchant having sailed on seventy-two voyages beyond Cape Maleus towards Italy, built a monument for himself and for his sons Flavius Theodoros and Flavius Theudas and for any others they may wish to grant permission to'.

being taken to trial in Rome (Acts 27). In such cases there was nothing that the pilot could do but to shelter in a port and wait for favourable weather.

Acts does not give any information about the kind of ships that the apostles embarked on during their sea journeys. Ancient literature, in addition to small coastal vessels, mentions the existence of large ships with the capacity of as many as six hundred passengers or more. Very different were the many small boats, that sailed along the coasts, coming into harbour each night. Such boats hopping from one port to the other, collected any kind of available passenger or merchandise. This practice is evident in the schedule of the boat on which Paul embarked on his journey to Rome as a prisoner; a boat 'bound for ports in the province of Asia' (Acts 27:2) which shortly after its departure from Caesarea stopped at Sidon.

On such coastal boats merchants, exiles, prostitutes or priests, all travelled together. As they made zigzags between islands and mainlands the travelling merchants would be collecting timber from Phoenicia, copper and wine from Cyprus, amphorae from Rhodes and Samos or grain mills from Cos. Such boats did not have a schedule and when the captain decided that his business was done and the wind was favourable he would send one of the crew to announce in the streets and taverns of the port that he was soon leaving. By the time that darkness fell unless he reached a port, he usually found a sheltered shallow bay and dropped anchor or beached his ships. Lifeboats were unknown. In case of danger, without the pilot there was no chance of survival. Paul, as an experienced traveller who claimed to have suffered three shipwrecks (2 Cor. 11:25) knew this well because when the vessel carrying him faced shipweck off Malta during his last journey and the crew tried to sneak off using the dinghy to save their own lives, he got the centurion and the soldiers and told them that unless those men stayed with the ship, they could not be saved (Acts 27:30-31). People also took passage on vessels carrying cargo. On the same ill-fated voyage, Paul embarked at Myra on one of the big grain vessels bound from Alexandria to Rome. We know from the words of Luke that this ship had 276 people aboard, counting the crew (Acts 27:37), but some took even more, the passengers sleeping on the open decks.

On boats such as this, or probably larger, would Paul have sailed the eastern Mediterranean, to carry Christ's message to Cyprus, Anatolia, and Greece.

TARSUS : CITY OF PAUL

At the time of Paul's birth and upbringing, Tarsus was the most important city in the Cilician plain (Çukurova) which was then known as Smooth Cilicia.[1]

When Paul was born, Tarsus was already very ancient. Excavations at Gözlü Kule tumulus in the present city have shown that this site was occupied since the Neolithic period, from about the seventh millennium BCE. During its later Bronze Age history the tumulus is thought to have been the capital of the kingdom of Kizzuwatna. The famous Hittite queen Puduhepa,[2] before she moved to the Hittite capital Hattusa, was a priestess in Kizzuwatna, whose capital was 'Tarsa'. The first Greek elements in the settlement's culture date from the beginning of the twelfth century BCE, the time of upheavals created by the Sea Peoples.

In Assyrian annals the tumulus appears as 'Tarzi', and the capital of the kingdom of Que (Cilician plain). The reference to Cilicia in the Second Book of Chronicles is related approximately to this period of the city's history in the tenth century BCE: 'Solomon also imported horses from Egypt and Cilicia. The king's agents would acquire them by purchase from Cilicia, and would then bring up chariots from Egypt and export them at six hundred silver shekels, with the horses going for a hundred and fifty shekels. At these rates they served as middlemen for all the Hittite and Aramean kings' (2 Chr 1:16-17).

King Sennacherib[3] (705-651 BCE) of Assyria, is known to have moved the city from the tumulus to its present location on the Cydnus river (Tarsus çayı) to a point some 15 km from the sea. Before reaching the Mediterranean Cydnus flowed into a large lagoon, which was known as the lake of Rhegma in Roman times, and was navigable up to the city. At present the area where this lake existed is a fertile cotton field. In the Old Testament, Tarshish, which frequently means 'ocean-going ships,' is used as a place-name in the Mediterranean after the sixth-fifth centuries BCE, from which metals like silver,

(opposite) Detail from a mosaic discovered in Tarsus. Third century CE. Hatay Archaeological Museum. Antakya. In a frame of waves and twisted ribbon it represents Orpheus among beasts. The mosaicist has enhanced the hero's costume with glass cubes in orange, green and blue. The technique and iconography of the mosaic shows that it may have been produced by the artists of the mosaics of Antioch on the Orontes.

[1] Cilicia Pedias. To the west of the plain rose the heavily forested mountains of Rough Cilicia (Cilicia Tracheia) which was infested with pirates and brigands until 67 BCE when Roman rule was established by general Pompey.

[2] Wife of Hattusili III (about 1275-1250 BCE) and mother of Tudhaliya IV.

[3] Failed to enter Jerusalem (701 BCE) and was smitten by the angel of the Lord (Is 37:21-36; 2 Kgs 19:20-35).

iron or lead came to Tyre in Phoenicia. Some scholars regard this place as being Tarsus,[4] the major port in Cilicia having connections with inland states of Anatolia rich in metals, horses and slaves: 'Tarshish traded with you, so great was your wealth, exchanging silver, iron, tin, and lead for your wares' (Ez 27:12). All of what was built in ancient Tarsus after its refoundation on the plain lies under the silt of the Cydnus river and the city's apartment houses, some 6 metres deep.

Following the collapse of the Assyrian kingdom, Cilicia seems to have survived as an independent state until Anatolia was captured by Cyrus the Great (555-530 BCE) of the Persian empire. Tarsus was the first urban centre with the amenities of civilization after crossing the Cilician Gates to the south, and thus an indispensable stage to recover before travelling on to Syria and the countries beyond. According to Xenophon, Cyrus the Younger, and to Arrian, Alexander the Great did not miss the chance of enjoying the opportunities the city offered. In *Anabasis*[5] Cyrus, after crossing the 'impassable' Cilician Gates (401 BCE) found himself in the large and well-watered Cilician plain 'full of all kinds of trees and of vines', which 'produces quantities of sesame and millet and wheat and barley', its capital 'a large and prosperous city' with a river called the Cydnus running 'through the middle of the city'. Strabo in *Geography* says that an immersion in the Cydnus was 'beneficial both to beasts and to men who suffer from sinews'. It is not known if Alexander knew this when he plunged into the river some four hundred years before Strabo, a venture which ended up immediately with acute pneumonia and almost cost him his life. Sometime after it came under Roman rule in 50 BCE the statesman Cicero is known to have served as the first Roman governor of Cilicia, staying at Tarsus. One of the most memorable events of the city's early Roman history, which was later commemorated by Shakespeare, was the love story of Mark Antony (Marcus Antonius) and Cleopatra which began here (41 BCE).

Some eight years before Cleopatra had had herself delivered to Caesar in Alexandria by a slave, wrapped in a carpet. This time she arranged a parade

(opposite) Uncovered section of the ancient street in Tarsus. It is thought to have been laid during the Seleucid restoration of the city in the mid-second century BCE. The road is paved with black basalt blocks sloping on the sides towards the drainage channels. It is also provided with a gutter. The ruins of a portico and halls flanking it are thought to date from the third-fourth centuries CE.

[4] The other candidate, as a place-name, is Tartessos in Spain.

[5] Cyrus the Younger marched from Sardis to Persia in order to dethrone his brother Artaxerxes. He would eventually lose the battle of Cunaxa (401 BCE) and be killed. *Anabasis* is the story of the trip of the 'Ten Thousand' Greek mercenaries who had joined Cyrus in this expediton, through eastern Anatolia and Black Sea to Greece.

which was exaggerated by later writers, but still appropriate to the vulgar and ambitious character of Antony. She had built for herself a barge with fittings in gold and silver and equipped with purple silk sails. The vessel's crew, young boys and girls, were dressed as Erotes and Nereids. The sound of music and scent of rich perfumes reached across the water to the Tarsians who had flocked to the Cydnus' banks. 'Cleopatra herself reclined beneath a canopy of cloth of gold.' This was the beginning of a love story which lasted about a decade, with the well-known fatal end. Among many things which Antony would bestow on his beloved after a few years were the cedar-rich mountains of Rough Cilicia, which was a major timber source of the Roman world for ship-building.

Recent excavations have shown that Tarsus was a smaller flourishing copy of Antioch on the Orontes during the Roman period. Rome had made it a 'free city'; it had its own governing body of citizens — responsible to the Roman governor — and was exempted from many taxes. A prosperous city in the first century, Paul's pride in his home is evident when he says 'I am a Jew, of Tarsus in Cilicia, a citizen of no mean city' (Acts 21:39). Acts mentions Paul's Tarsus citizenship only twice (Acts 21:39; 22:3) and does not give any information about it. However, since owning this status cost some money one may conclude that Paul's family was wealthy. The ancient street which has recently been excavated, the remains of the Via Tauris connecting the city to the Cilician Gates and the large floor mosaic which was brought to light in the city (displayed at Hatay Archaeological Museum in Antakya) give us an idea about the Tarsus of the Roman period.

When he begins his defence before the king Herod Agrippa II (50-100), Paul makes it clear that he spent all his youth among Jews in Jerusalem (Acts 26:4) having been sent there to study under Gamaliel[6] (Acts 22:3). Although ancient literature refers to Tarsus as a seat of Greek philosophy, famous for its Stoic school, it is known that Paul, having spent most of his youth in Jerusalem, did not have the chance to make use of this opportunity. Paul returned to his native city to teach the gospel, before he was fetched by Barnabas from Antioch. Though not explicitly stated in Acts it seems likely that he visited his city again when he travelled to Galatia and Pisidia during his second and third journeys.

[6] Perhaps Gamaliel I who was known as the leading Pharisee teacher of the period (Acts 5:34).

"I am a Jew, of Tarsus in Cilicia, a citizen of no mean city" (Acts 21:39).

ANTIOCH ON THE ORONTES : HEADQUARTERS OF THE GENTILE MISSION

Antioch on the Orontes (Antakya), once called the 'Queen of the East' and known as the third largest city of the Roman empire, played a pivotal role in the spread of Christianity from Palestine to the Diaspora.

On the main trade routes from the east to the Mediterranean and from Syria to Anatolia this prosperous city was founded by Seleucus I Nicator about 300 BCE. Seleucus I's father Antiochus was one of the generals of Alexander the Great and inherited the largest portion of Alexander's lands after the latter's death. His kingdom's frontiers extended from the Hellespont to India. 'Orontes' was attached to city's name to distinguish it from the other fifteen more Antiochs which this king is said to have founded,[1] naming all of them after his father. Among its foundation stories the one which does justice to the character of the later Antiochenes, who seem in course of time to have cultivated a great number of harmless vanities, is probably the one constructed by the people of the city of the present day. According to this, a king who suffered from insomnia came to the slope of Mt Silpius in his search to find a place which would help him to fall asleep. Here, to the suprise of his family and retinue he descended from his horse, lay on the grass, put his head on a piece of stone and started snoring. After waking up he decided that this was the right spot for his new city.

Limited excavation and fairly extensive ancient sources provide the evidence for our knowledge of the ancient city. It was laid out between the Orontes (Asi) river and Mt Silpius (Habib Neccar Dağı) and surrounded by a wall. It was founded on the grid plan, which was the fashion of the period and possessed all the indispensable institutions of a *polis*.

With the decline of the Seleucid power the city became a prey for Tigranes I of Armenia (95-64 BCE) for a short period and then in 64 BCE was taken over by Rome, to be made the capital of the province of Syria which would be established a few years later.

Among its monuments Antioch's fame came from the great colonnaded street which ran from east to west along the walls of the earlier city. By the

---

[1] Tarsus was also refounded by the same king as Antioch on the Cydnus.

Personification of Antioch on the Orontes in *Tabula Peutingeriana* (Peutinger Map). It is shown as a woman seated on a throne holding a spear in her right hand. Her head is nimbed. The name of the city, 'Antiochia' is divided into two by her head. Her left hand rests on the head of the god of the Orontes river, personified as a young nude boy. Water pours out of the vessel which he holds in his left hand and flows by an aqueduct towards a pool covered by a building in the grove of Daphne (Defne). Seleucia Pieria (Çevlik), Rhosos (Arsuz), Alexandretta (İskenderun) and Epiphania can be distinguished.

time it was completed, in the reign of Tiberius (14-37 CE) the 10 metre-wide marble-paved street, with pavements totalling the same width, was flanked by roofed double-storeyed colonnades, making it possible to walk for 4 km under porticoes. It was known as one of the earliest of such kind of main streets.

The city was founded in the major earthquake zone and there was regular rebuilding under both its Hellenistic and Roman rulers. During an earthquake in 115 CE, the emperor Trajan, who was then staying in the city, saved his life by jumping out of a window of his palace. Though almost nothing is left of this once great city, the stunning mosaics brought to light from the excavations in Antioch, its suburbs, Daphne (Defne) and Seleucia Pieria (Çevlik) give at least some idea of the prosperity and high living standard of ancient Antioch.[2]

By Paul's time the city was already spreading towards the level plain to the south of the Orontes river which Strabo claims to have been navigable until it reached the Mediterranean. Pausanias, however, states that the river 'does not flow throughout its whole course to the sea on level ground, but tumbles over a precipitous ledge of rock. Wishing, then, that ships should sail up the river from the sea to the city of Antioch, the Roman emperor [thought to be Vespasian] had a navigable canal dug with much labour and at great expense, and into this canal he diverted the river.' The information about the work of Vespasian shows the importance that the Romans afforded to the Orontes as a communication route from the Mediterranean to the city and Syria.

Agricultural produce was bountiful in the warm climate and its position on trade routes, notably the silk route, helped to make this an extremely wealthy city, attracting traders and artists from many countries. The inhabitants of city according to Tacitus 'enjoyed having dealings with the soldiers they knew, and many of the provincials were linked with them by marriage and family ties.' The Roman soldiers who were based at the camps near Antioch were known to have been reluctant to leave the region. The wealth and luxury of the

---

[2] Displayed at Hatay Archaeological Museum in Antakya, the Louvre and over twenty museums or galleries in the USA.

city were famed and the sybaritic, self indulgent lifestyle of its inhabitants was immortalised by the first-century Roman satirist Juvenal, commenting on the effect of oriental excesses on Roman life:

'For years now Syrian Orontes has poured its sewerage into our native Tiber-
Its lingo and manners, its flutes, its outlandish harps
With their transverse strings, its native tambourines,
And the whores who hang out round the race-course.'

Visiting the city some three hundred years later the Byzantine emperor Julian the Apostate (361-63) could not help himself from dwelling on, among many other vanities, on the greed, effeminacy or laziness of the Antiochenes.

The earliest inhabitants of the city were the Macedonian veterans in the Seleucid army, immigrants from Greece and Jews. In the first century CE the city's population was more than 200,000 of which perhaps more than one fifth were Jews. In general, the Jews of Antioch were wealthy and since Seleucid times had enjoyed almost all the rights of full citizenship to the chagrin of non-Jewish citizens; in contrast to the Jews of Palestine, they were not riven by factions. Most were Greek-speaking and used the Septuagint, the Greek translation of the Torah (the first five books of the Old Testament). Judaism's monotheism and its ethical teachings for the conduct of life, together with the fact that Greek was spoken in the synagogues, 'regularly attracted large numbers of Greeks to their worship, and they had, to some degree, made them a part of their community.'

To this cosmopolitan city, with its Greek and oriental cults and philosophies, came Hellenistic Jewish Christians, fleeing the persecutions of Jerusalem that had been responsible for the death of Stephen in about 34. When the Jerusalem church heard that plenty of Gentiles had 'turned to the Lord' they sent Barnabas to Antioch. It is not known how long the apostle worked here. However, when he saw that he needed asistance he went to Tarsus and fetched Paul. From the words used by Luke 'when he found Paul' one may conclude that the apostle, having been rejected by his co-citizens was not there but proclaiming the gospel in the countryside. Within a few years, perhaps by about 40, following the popular practice of the time to refer to the partisans of a famous person as

'For a whole year they met with the church and taught a large number of people, and it was in Antioch that the disciples were first called Christians' (Acts 11:26).

Detail from the border of the Yakto mosaic from Daphne. Mid-fifth century CE. Hatay Archaeological Museum. Antakya. Although it dates some four hundred years after Paul's time the mosaic reflects the monuments and life in Roman Antioch. In front of 'the laboratory [workshop] of Martyrion' a servant pours wine for his master. Next is a group of a man, an elderly woman, and a young woman, who holds an object in her left hand, in familiar conversational gestures. A young boy holding a basket is in front of 'the Olympic Stadium'.

'Herodians' or 'Pompeians' (supporters or clients of Pompey), the term Christians,[3] a Greek word with a Latin adjectival ending, first came into use (Acts 11:26), originating in the city to describe the Greek-speaking Gentile followers of Christ, as distinct from the Jews. The new term comprised all the known terms used until then to refer to the believers of the new faith: brethren, witnesses, those of the way, saints etc. The coinage of the word also shows that at the beginning Christianity was regarded as a sort of semi-political movement.

For many years, this multi-cultural city was the main base and focal point of their missionary activity amongst the Gentiles. It is a measure of the success of their mission, that during the severe famine (45-47), the Antiochene community sent aid to the believers in Jerusalem.

Peter too was associated with Antioch, having been there at the time of Paul and Barnabas; according to one tradition, he is regarded as the founder of the church of Antioch and even its first bishop. A cave on the slope of Mt Staurin,[4] the eastern extension of Mt Silpius, is traditionally regarded as a meeting place of the early Christians. The grotto was given a façade, probably in the eleventh century after the crusader conquest, since which time it has been the church of Peter. Also, an Eastern tradition holds that the Gospel of Matthew was recorded in this city.

There is nothing left to be seen from Paul's time in Antioch. If there was one sight that the apostle could not have missed during his frequent stays in the city, this must have been the giant relief situated next to the grotto of Peter. Ancient literature relates that in the reign of Antiochus I (281-261 BCE) to protect Antioch from a plague a 'philosopher and wonder-worker' named Laiios commanded the carving of a great mask with some special words on it for the salvation of the city. The talisman was called by the people of Antioch 'Charonion'. On its right shoulder a smaller figure was carved.

[3] Greek *christianoi*, 'Christians' or 'Christus-people'.

[4] Mountain of the Cross. Named thus after a cross which appeared in the sky above the mountain following an earthquake in the sixth century CE.

'While they were worshiping the Lord and fasting, the holy Spirit said, "Set apart for me Barnabas and Saul for the work to which I have called them" ' (Acts 13:2).

Next to the stadium is the 'Private bath of Ardabourious' which consists of two gabled buildings linked by a construction with a pyramidal roof and with some trees in its garden. The owner of the bath held the office of *magister militum per orientem* in Antioch (450-57 CE). To the left are a rider and his servant as he turns his head backwards clearing the way for his patron; to the right is a man with a basket in his outstretched hand and a bundle under his left arm, perhaps about to enter the bath.

SELEUCIA PIERIA : PORT OF ANTIOCH ON THE ORONTES

Seleucia (in) Pieria was founded partly on a rocky promontory projecting from Mt Coryphaeus and partly on the small plain below, some 10 km away from the point where the Orontes river pours into the Mediterranean at the foot of Mt Casius (Keldağ). In the archives of Ugarit and to the Hittites[1] this mountain was known as Mt Hazzi. According to legend, while Seleucus I (321-281 BCE) was sacrificing on this mountain an eagle snatched part of the sacrificial offering and carried it to the place where the new town would be built. It was named after the nearby Mt Pieria (Musa Dağı). Seleucia Pieria (Çevlik) was chosen as a capital before the foundation of Antioch and was one of the nine cities which the king had named after his dynasty. The king, however, seeing that a coastal city was open to attacks from the sea, and lacking a strong navy, preferred to move the new capital of his kingdom to Antioch from where the inland trade routes also could be controlled. His worries would later be confirmed by the occupation of the port by Ptolemies of Egypt between 241-219 BCE, which is mentioned in the First Book of Maccabees: 'Plotting evil against Alexander, King Ptolemy took possession of the cities along the seacoast as far as Seleucia-by-the-Sea' (1 Mc 11:8).

The port of Seleucia was created by enlarging a natural basin formed by a stream. Later, under Vespasian and then Titus, and Domitian and finally completed in the following century, an artificial watercourse was constructed to divert this stream from the harbour to prevent it from being silted up. This is a canal of some 1400 m long, the final 130 m of which was tunnelled through the rock to a height and width of 6 m. The cutting of so-called tunnel of Titus was the greatest project that Rome ever undertook in the provinces. Inscriptions which have survived on its walls, and which give the names of Vespasian (69-79) and Titus (79-81), originally must have also included Domitian (81-96). Other inscriptions record that the work was done in sections and by the participation of particular Roman legions stationed in eastern Anatolia. Some inscriptions also show that further work was done by soldiers of the legions under Antoninus Pius in about 149.

This was the port from which the apostles Paul, Barnabas and John Mark sailed to Cyprus and beyond on their first missionary journey.

(opposite) Commemorative inscription from the wall of the tunnel of Titus in Seleucia Pieria. First century CE. In Latin it reads 'Divine Vespasian and Divine Titus made it'. The indecipherable word in the lower right corner must have been a later addition in Greek.

[1] One of the reliefs in the rock-sanctuary of Yazılıkaya near Hattusa depicts the Hittite storm-god Teshup standing on the deified mountains of Namni and Hazzi.

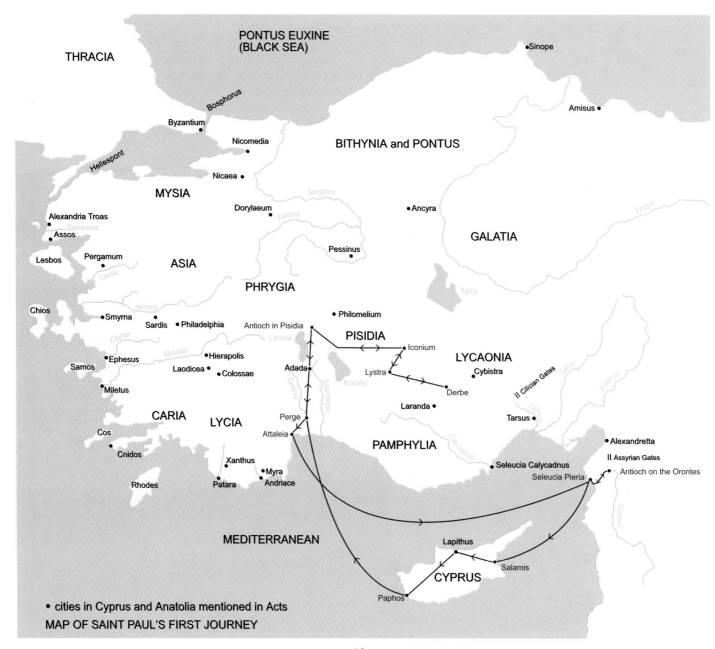

MAP OF SAINT PAUL'S FIRST JOURNEY

THRACIA

PONTUS EUXINE (BLACK SEA)

• Sinope

Amisus •

Bosphorus

• Byzantium

• Nicomedia

BITHYNIA and PONTUS

Hellespont

MYSIA

• Nicaea

Sangarius

• Dorylaeum

Tembris

• Ancyra

• Alexandria Troas

Satnioeis

• Assos

Lesbos

• Pergamum

Calcus

ASIA

PHRYGIA

Hermus

GALATIA

Tatta

Pessinus •

Halys

Chios

• Smyrna

• Sardis

• Philadelphia

Cayster

Meander

Limnai

• Philomelium

Antioch in Pisidia •

PISIDIA

• Iconium

LYCAONIA

• Cybistra

II Cilician Gates

Pyramus

• Ephesus

Samos

• Hierapolis

Laodicea •

• Colossae

Adada •

Cestus

Eurymedon

Koralis

Lystra •

• Derbe

Sarus

Miletus •

CARIA

LYCIA

Perge •

Attaleia •

PAMPHYLIA

• Laranda

Calycadnus

Tarsus •

Cydnus

• Alexandretta

II Assyrian Gates

• Cos

• Cnidos

Xanthus •

• Myra

Patara •

Andriace •

MEDITERRANEAN

Seleucia Calycadnus •

Seleucia Pieria

Antioch on the Orontes

Orontes

Rhodes

Lapithus •

CYPRUS

Salamis •

Paphos •

• cities in Cyprus and Anatolia mentioned in Acts

MAP OF SAINT PAUL'S FIRST JOURNEY

PAUL'S FIRST JOURNEY

Antioch on the Orontes — Seleucia Pieria — Salamis — Paphos — Perge — Antioch in Pisidia — Iconium — Lystra — Derbe — Lystra — Iconium — Antioch in Pisidia — Perge — Attaleia — Seleucia Pieria — Antioch on the Orontes

In the spring of the year 45 Paul set out on their first missionary journey from Antioch on the Orontes. His travel companions were Barnabas and John Mark.

Barnabas' background, as both a Levite, namely a member of a Jewish priestly family, descended from Aaron, the brother of Moses and a Hellenistic Jew from the Diaspora, was not dissimilar to Paul's. He could speak Greek and was familiar with pagans. It was Barnabas who had gone from Antioch to Tarsus, found Paul and explained him what was being asked from them. Barnabas also had introduced Paul to Peter and James, the Lord's brother and related them Paul's story. These were the only apostles Paul ever met. John Mark, a cousin of Barnabas, probably owed his participancy in the journey as the third member of the group to James. If John Mark was the young man who had followed Jesus into the Garden of Gethsemane 'wearing nothing but a linen cloth' and who left his garment 'behind and ran off naked' (Mk 14:51), he must have met Jesus Christ and knew his life and thus could help the preaching of his companions as an eyewitness.

Although the distance between Antioch and Seleucia was no more than 15 km as the bird flies, the region was rugged and overland transportation was very difficult. The apostles probably sailed downstream by the Orontes to reach Seleucia, which must have taken a day. There, according to the fifth-century apocryphal Acts of Barnabas they had to wait for three days to find a ship bound to Cyprus. The memory of the missionaries' departure must have lingered for a long time because during the previous century each of the two piers of the outer harbour of the city, until they disappeared under water, was named after Paul and Barnabas.

Cyprus, the island to which their first journey took them was situated at the centre of the eastern Mediterranean had been a kind of crossroads of ancient civilizations. Barnabas was a native of Salamis and would have known the island well, hence perhaps the decision to come here.

The island's earliest inhabitants are thought to have been immigrants from Syrian and Cilician coasts. On clear days the silhouette of the Troodos chain of Cyprus is visible from these countries; and thus small rafts must have been

So they, sent forth by the holy Spirit, went down to Seleucia and from there sailed to Cyprus (Acts 13:4).

Remains of the dock of ancient harbour of Seleucia Pieria. In the background is the silhouette of Mt Casius.

sufficient to take the first inhabitants there.

The rich copper deposits of the island are thought to have been utilized since the beginning of the Bronze Age, sometime around 3000 BCE, and have given the island its name.[1] Ox-hide copper ingots brought to light by underwater archaeology indicate that, in addition to agricultural produce such as wine, corn and olive oil, this metal was the most important source of wealth for the islanders. Being on ancient trade routes the island was influenced by the Anatolian cultures, and the civilizations of Mesopotamia, Egypt, Crete, Greece and Sicily. Kition, its capital and the most flourishing city of the Bronze Age is thought to be the Alasiya mentioned in Hittite cuneiform tablets. The Old Testament term 'kittim' referred to the inhabitants of this city and was later used for Cypriots in general and eventually for Greeks and even Romans. Like Anatolia, Greece, the Aegean islands and the eastern Levant, in about

[1] Greek *kypros,* 'copper'.

1200 BCE Cyprus suffered the destruction of the Sea Peoples. Some of these immigrants may have also settled on the island. The strongest Greek element introduced to the ancient culture of Cyprus dates to this period. When Cyprus recovered from the Dark Age (about 1200-800 BCE) it was ruled successively by the Assyrians, Phoenicians, Egyptians and Persians.

The Greek city states which were established on the island took a short respite after the conquest of Alexander's navy in 333 BCE. Meanwhile Petra tou Romiou,[2] some 20 km to the southeast of Paphos, had traditionally become the place where the goddess Aphrodite was born from foam.[3] During the Hellenistic era the island was under the hegemony of the Ptolemies of Egypt which ended in 58 BCE with the conquest of Rome. Thus, at the time that the apostles' ship sailed into the harbour of Salamis the island was a part of the Roman empire with a Roman governor.

Although the Romans had chosen Paphos for the residency of the proconsul, Salamis was still the most important city in Cyprus. At the time that Paul, Barnabas and Mark entered the city it boasted the institutions of a large Hellenistic *polis*: a theater and a gymnasium both of which were being enlarged during this period.

At Salamis, where there was a large Jewish community, known to have moved to the island after Augustus leased the salt mines to king Herod the Great (37-4 BCE). The first believers were also some Jews who had to leave Jerusalem when the persecutions began (Acts 11:19). In Acts, one of the Cypriot converts is mentioned as 'Mnason, a Cypriot, a disciple of long standing' at whose house Paul would stay in Jerusalem when he returned from his third journey (Acts 21:16).

There is not any information about the content of the apostles' message in Cyprus but that they proclaimed the word of God in the synagogues. The fifth-century apocryphal Acts of Barnabas mentions a synagogue which was 'near the place called biblia, where Barnabas, having unrolled the gospel which he had received from Matthew his fellow-labourer, began to teach Jews.' Excavations in Salamis have not yet brought to light any synagogue of Paul's era or later. All of the early synagogues must have been destroyed following

'When they arrived in Salamis, they proclaimed, the word of God in the Jewish synagogues' (Acts 13:5).

[2] The name means 'Stone of the Romans', for the Greeks of the Byzantine era designated themselves as *Romaioi*, 'Romans'.

[3] Greek *aphros*, 'foam'.

the big Jewish revolt which began in Egypt and spread to the island (115-17). When the rebellion was suppressed 'no Jew was allowed to appear on the island' by the order of the emperor Trajan.

From Salamis the apostles travelled across the island or 'through the whole island' (Acts 13:6) to Paphos. The expression, probably, is used to imply that in addition to those of Salamis and Paphos, some of the other Jewish communities were visited. The trip would have been made either by following the coast or transversing the island. During the apostles' calls the Cypriots probably knew more about Barnabas whom they later regarded as their patron saint, than Paul. His given name, Barnabas (from Hebrew *barnebhuah*=son of 'prophecy'), may infer a role as a prophet or teacher. Previously in Jerusalem, he had 'sold a piece of property that he owned, then brought the money at the feet of the apostles' (Acts 4:37). In Acts his name is interpreted by Luke as 'son of consolation'.

The apocryphal Acts of Barnabas states that they visited Lapithus (Lapta) along the northern coast of the island where they were not received well because of the 'idol festival' which was being celebrated then. They continued 'through the mountains and came to the city of Lampadistus' which is now identified with the resort of Kalopanayiotis village some 70 km to the southwest of the island's present capital. During their wanderings they had to take refuge in 'the village of the Ledrians' from the Jews who opposed them and were looking for them. Ledra is the ancient name of Nicosia (Lefkoşe). From there they possibly travelled south to Curium and Limassol and continued on the Roman road to Paphos.

In New Paphos, where a well-established Jewish community is thought to have existed, the apostles were summoned to speak in the presence of Sergius Paulus, the Roman governor who had a Jewish sorcerer named Elymas Bar-Jesus. During this period employment of magicians or sorcerers by rich people was popular; worshipping one or more gods or cults was common. As he had shown interest in what Elymas represented, he wanted to hear about the cult of the new speaker. To the magician, Paul must have appeared as a rival and he tried to prevent his patron from hearing the apostle's preaching. Paul, calling upon the power of the Holy Spirit, temporarily struck blind the sorcerer. This miracle so impressed the governor that when he 'saw what had happened he came to believe, for he was astonished by the teaching about the Lord' (Acts 13:12).

(opposite) Palaestra of the gymnasium of Salamis. Augustan period (27 BCE - 14 CE).

"You son of devil, you enemy of all that is right, full of every sort of deceit and froud. Will you not stop twisting the straight paths of [the] Lord?" (Acts 13:10).

Paul seems to have employed the method which would have been used by any magician of the time. Fixing his eyes on his opponent, he cursed him so that Bar-Jesus, at least temporarily, lost his eyesight. It has been suggested that the phrase may refer to 'spiritual blindness' which later led to the story of 'actual blindness'. One may also infer that the blinding of the magician, a false prophet, opened the governor's eyes. The conversion of Sergius Paulus, however, could not have had an immediate role on the spread of Christianity in the island, because proconsuls were usually appointed for one year periods and there was no reason why the Cypriots should follow the religion of the Roman administrator.

From this point on, in Acts, the apostle is not referred to as Saul, but Paul. Early Christian writings suggest that the apostle changed his name after this famous conversion. Nevertheless, choosing Greek names was not unusual among Jews even before the time of Paul and it did not necessarily indicate a hellenizing tendency.[4] It has been also claimed that here the change of the apostle's name refers to a change in his role; from being a Jew among Jews in the Semitic world of Palestine, to a Roman citizen in the hall of a Roman proconsul,[5] in the Gentile world. Thus his ancient royal name had lost its importance. This governor, however, is said to have been Lucius Sergius Paulus a native of Antioch in Pisidia who later became a consul in Rome. It is probable that he suggested Paul should go to Antioch in Pisidia where he had relatives and estates and even gave him letters of introduction.

A Cypriot legend maintains that the apostles were imprisoned and scourged in Paphos before their encounter with the governor. A broken column in the former church of Chrysopolitissa (also known as of St Kriake) near New Paphos is said to have been used to tie up Paul and lash him 39 times. The tradition of 'columns of flagellations' seems to have been inspired by Paul's words that five times at the hand of the Jews he was scourged 'forty lashes minus one' (2 Cor 11:24). According to the book of Deuteronomy forty stripes, but no more, may be given to a man whom the judge found guilty, in order

Church built over the tomb of St Barnabas near Salamis.

<hr>

[4] The most famous hellenized personage of the period — though half-Jewish — was king Herod the Great, who chose the name 'Agrippa' for his successors after the Roman general Marcus Agrippa who was friendly to Jews. Later, Paul would defend himself in front of king Agrippa II (50-100) (Acts 26).

[5] Latin *pro consule*, 'proconsul'.

Icon of St Barnabas. Twentieth century. St Barnabas Museum. North Cyprus.

'From Paphos, Paul and his companions set sail and arrived at Perga in Pamphylia' (Acts 13:13).

not to disagrace his relatives 'because of the severity of the beating' (Dt 25:2-3). With the standards of the time this was regarded as a mild punishment. It has also been suggested that the expression, probably, did not refer to the number of strokes but the type of whip, which had 39 cords tied in three bands of thirteen cords. The story in Paphos might have even been inspired by the incident in Jerusalem when the centurion gave instructions for the interrogation of Paul under the lash (Acts 22:24).

After a few years Barnabas returned to his island together with his cousin John Mark. There is no scriptural record about the return of Barnabas to Cyprus. Tradition has it that he was martyred in his native city Salamis probably about 61 and secretly buried. His reputed tomb was discovered in 489 in the reign of the emperor Zeno together with the manuscript of the Gospel according to Mark, placed on his chest by its author and a small church was built over it. A local tradition holds that the apostle was killed by the Jews who were incited by Elymas.

From Cyprus the apostles sailed to Perge in Pamphylia. This sea voyage may have taken about three days. Pamphylia was a narrow coastal plain between the Taurus chain and the Mediterranean extending from Cilicia to the heights of Lycia. It had been settled by a people of Anatolian origin and later by Greeks. The latter began to settle here after the great migrations around 1200 BCE and chose Trojan heroes as their ancestors. Amongst its prosperous cities were, in addition to Perge, Attaleia (Antalya), Side and Coracesium (Alanya).

Perge may have been the destination of the ship's captain, a situation with which the apostles seem to have complied. The Cestrus river (Aksu) that ran by the east of Perge, having no delta, was navigable from the sea and the apostles' vessel sailed or towed against the slow moving current up to the city, which by the middle of the first century had began moving from the original settlement on the acropolis to the flat plain.

At the time of Paul's arrival Perge was entering an era of great prosperity. Most of the standing remains are of a later date, but the walls, theatre and the circular Hellenistic towers of the main gate were there when the apostles came to this city. If one walked on the main street to the north one would have reached the palaestra, dedicated to the emperor Claudius (41-54). Later, in the early second century CE, the oval area flanked by the towers was converted into a beautiful marble-lined courtyard with niches housing statues of the gods,

the family of the emperor, the mythical founders of the city and various celebrities. Paul would certainly have seen the temple of Artemis of Perge which was described by Strabo as being 'near Perge on a lofty site, to the temple where a general festival is celebrated every year'.

Apart from Paul's brief visits and his preaching here, little is known about early Christianity in Perge. The apocyrphal Acts of Barnabas mentions a two-month stay in Perge. Here John Mark left them to return to Jerusalem. In Acts there is no indication why John Mark left. It has been suggested that he may have been jealous of Paul who by then had assumed the leadership of the party. It is also claimed that Paul's plans to bring the gospel to Gentiles may have been regarded unacceptable by John Mark. Or was he shocked and lost heart when he saw Paul all of a sudden sick? If this sickness were epilepsy, seeing the apostle with his eyes rolled up and foam at his mouth which had to be gagged and his body rigid as stone may have disappointed the young man. Whatever happened in Perge, the event affected Paul's faith in John Mark (Acts 15:36-41), although it did not affect his feelings towards Barnabas. Paul and John Mark were eventually reconciled, for many years later in his letter to the Colossians, Paul wrote 'Mark the cousin of Barnabas (concerning whom you have received instructions; if he comes to you, receive him)' (Col 4:10) and in his second letter to Timothy (4:11) which he wrote from the prison in Rome, 'Get Mark and bring him with you, for he is helpful to me in the ministry'.

Some scholars believe that the reason for Paul's moving to Pisidia and southern Galatia was the malaria he contracted, perhaps in his childhood. This would not have been surprising for his hometown and the rest of the Cilician plain were infested with mosquitos. Otherwise, for winning new converts the cosmopolitan coastal cities of Pamphylia were certainly more favourable than the scarcely populated northern highlands. Later when the apostle says 'you know that it was because of a physical illness that I originally preached the gospel to you, and you did not show disdain or contempt because of the trial caused by my physical condition, but rather you received me as an angel of God, as Jesus Christ' (Gal 4:13-14) he refers to his sickness. Whatever his sickness[6] was, the apostle's words make it clear that fresh mountain air was better for it than the hot and humid coastal plain.

(opposite) Relief with the Triumph of Dionysus from the theatre at Perge. Second century CE. It shows Dionysus seated on a chariot drawn by tigers and flanked by a satyr and a maenad.

"It was because of a physical illness that I originally preached the gospel to you" (Gal 4:13).

[6] Scholars suggest epilepsy, malaria, depression, failing eyesight and others as Paul's sickness.

The narrow passes of the Taurus chain were closed through the winter months, and thus the apostles are thought to have begun journeying north before snow began falling. Shortly after coming out of Perge the main Roman road was split into two and the path which turned to west crossed the mountains to the north of Attaleia and continued northwest towards Laodicea. If Paul took this longer road to reach Antioch in Pisidia he would have probably travelled to Cremna and Sagalassus, and ended up on the Via Sebaste which encircled the lakes Koralis (Beyşehir) and Limnai (Eğridir) to the north. Paul, however, eager both to leave the humid plain as quickly as possible, and reach his destination where he expected to make new Gentile converts, very probably took the second much shorter route. This road connected Perge to Antioch in Pisidia by way of Adada following the path of the Cestrus river, by a route which was used until recently by nomads and because of the high number of crossings is known in Turkish as 'Kırk Geçitler', 'Forty Passes'. The uncountable number of crossings on the ravine must have been a very difficult experience, for when Paul later says 'on frequent journeys, in dangers from rivers, dangers from robbers' (2 Cor 11:26), he is thought to allude to this part of his travels, to the deep gorges of Cestrus, dangerous even in autumn when dry. Adada was the most important ancient city on this route to Antioch in Pisidia and is still known by the local villagers as 'Karabavlu', 'Black Paul'[7] perhaps after a church dedicated to him.

On such a rugged track their trip may have taken about ten days or more to reach inland. A few decades before the Romans had pacified the Pisidian heights. Despite this, the apostles probably joined a group of travellers going in the same direction, and waited until a crowd big enough to discourage the bandits from attacking them was gathered. John Mark may even have worried about the brigands who haunted the Pisidian heights when he left the party.

Having lost the battle of Magnesia (190 BCE) against Rome, the Seleucids had retreated to the south of the Taurus mountains and the Seleucid hegemony in the north was taken over by the Galatians, who ruled as a vassal kingdom of Rome. This lasted until their last king Amyntas' (37-25 BCE) death, when the region was made a Roman province. With the exception of Derbe, the

(opposite) A section of the Roman road climbing the mountain just before entering Adada by which most probably Paul travelled to Pisidia and Galatia and back during his first missionary journey.

[7] Vernacular Turkish combines the word 'kara' with 'papaz', literally 'black' with 'priest' ('Paul'), inspired from the black habits of the Greek Orthodox priest class, unless Karabavlu derived from the Greek *Ayo Pavlo*, Saint Paul.

three cities Paul visited in this region (Antioch in Pisidia, Iconium, Lystra) were Roman colonies. They were settled by Italian war veterans and immigrants who brought with them their native political and social institutions. Their function was to guard the Roman military routes against the Pisidian mountain tribes.

Antioch in Pisidia (Yalvaç) lies on the slope of a mountain overlooking a fertile valley northeast of lake Limnai, by the river Anthius (Yalvaç çayı). The city was probably founded by Seleucus I (321-281 BCE) and again named after his father Antiochus. It was called 'Antioch ad Pisidiam', 'Antioch in ('towards' or 'next to') Pisidia' in order to distinguish it from a number of Antiochs that the king had founded. Near the Phrygian and Pisidian borders, the city was settled with Macedonian soldiers. The population was doubtless expanded by local Phrygians, as the city's main deities were Anatolian: Cybele the Great Mother, whose main sanctuary lay north at Pessinus, and the moon god Men, to whom numerous votives were offered by Antiochenes at his temple at the top of a nearby mountain at Karakuyu.

Antioch in Pisidia was an important city for the Romans during their war with the Homonadeis, a people who had preyed on the Pisidian heights and the first colony in the region, named Colonia Caesarea Antiocheia. The pacification of the Pisidian heights was achieved by the consul Publius Sulpicius Quirinius who is said to have left no man free in the countryside and forced the younger generation to adopt Roman customs. By 6 BCE the Taurus range had become quiet and the consul was transferred to Syria, which he was to govern, and to hold the great census at the time when Jesus Christ was born in Bethlehem (Lk 2:1-7).

Some scholars think that although physical pre-occupations may explain Paul's preference of preaching the gospel to the people in the cool heights (Gal 4:13) rather those in the damp and hot Pamphylian lowlands, this is not enough to explain why he did not go from Perge to any of the better-populated and better-situated cities such as Sagalassus or Cremna but turned directly towards Antioch in Pisidia.

Antioch's elite families were descended from the Italian colonists and one of them was a relative of the proconsul of Cyprus, Sergius Paulus who had been converted to Christianity by Paul a few months ago. It is possible that this contact, with all the possibilities it suggested, was one of the reasons for the apostle's visit to Antioch in Pisidia where he hoped to make similar highly-placed converts. Iulius Sergius Paullus, whose name is encountered on a stone

(opposite) Votive reliefs and inscriptions from the outer wall of the sanctuary of the Anatolian moon god Men Askaenos at Karakuyu near Antioch in Pisidia. Each gabled rectangle probably imitates the architecture of the shrine which housed the god's statue and at its centre has a crescent moon, the symbol of Men. The temple was one of the most important Anatolian shrines when Paul was there.

discovered at Antioch[8] is believed to be the son or grandson of Sergius Paulus of Cyprus.

Although the city was the largest in the region there is no information about the size of the Jewish community. The evidence of the existence of a Jewish people in the area comes from a second- or third-century-CE epitaph found in Apollonia (Uluborlu) which refers to a Jewess named Debbora, a citizen of Antioch, married to a man from Sillyum in Pamphylia who is thought to have settled in Apollina. This epitaph says that Debbora was 'born of renowned parents'. The name is, however, Semitic and implies that her 'renowned parents' probably lived in Antioch on the Orontes rather than Antioch in Pisidia.

When the apostles entered the synagogue,[9] they sat down with the rest of the congregation and prayed. After the prayers and the readings they were invited to address the assembly. According to Jewish custom, as Jesus had done before (Lk 4:16), a person was free to speak in the synagogue (Acts 17:1-2). Paul shared his knowledge of the Scriptures and his belief in the death and resurrection of Jesus with his audience. After delivering his address here Paul was invited to preach on the next Sabbath. When, subsequently, Paul drew a large crowd of Jews and Gentiles, some Jewish members of the regular congregation became angry and their reaction made the apostles say 'It was necessary that the word of god be spoken you first, but since you reject it and condemn yourself as unworthy of eternal life, we now turn to the Gentiles' (Acts 13:48).

The Gentiles were happy to hear Paul's message but the Jewish listeners 'incited the women of prominence who were worshipers and the leading men of the city, stirred up a persecution against Paul and Barnabas, and expelled them from their territory' (Acts 13:50).

Paul might have hoped that not only Jews, but also Gentiles from important families who were Jewish sympathizers, and so sometimes attended the synagogue, would perhaps accept his Christian message. In the event, it was to the Jews of Antioch rather than to Paul, that these well-connected people gave support and the apostles were persecuted and expelled from Antioch. When he later speaks about his sufferings and says 'Three times I was beaten with rods' (2 Cor 11:25), a magistrate's punishment with the

(opposite) Remains of the imperial temple dedicated to Augustus (27 BCE-14 CE) at Antioch in Pisidia. Its podium was cut from the living rock of the mountain. The scattered white blocks belonged to its superstructure. The temple was partly encircled by a rock-cut portico of two storeys as the beam holes imply. Its construction was still going on when Paul visited the city.

'For so the Lord has commanded us, "I have made you a light to the Gentiles, that you may be an instrument of salvation to the ends of the earth" ' (Acts 13:47).

[8] Yalvaç Museum.

[9] Greek *synagoge*, as it is used in Acts, may refer to a 'building' or 'assembly'.

rods of Roman lictors, one of the cases may have been here at Antioch in Pisidia.

Nevertheless, some converts were made, and although their number may not have been high it was the first time a church of Gentiles isolated from the Jewish community was established. It was probably this fact which kindled the anger of the local Jews against the apostles.

Paul and Barnabas returned here from Iconium before going on to Perge 'Confirming the souls of the disciples and exhorting them to continue in the faith' (Acts 14:22). It is very probable that Paul came here in the course of his second and third journeys because the region was on his way to the province of Asia, Macedonia and Greece.

Almost none of the ruins which can be seen today, probably with the exception of the aqueduct which brought water from a spring 10 km north, were here when Paul came. The temple of Augustus and Tiberius' courtyard with the street leading to it were under construction.

Thus 'shaking the dust from their feet' so as not no be defiled by a heathen community the apostles left. The expression has been used by Christ in his teaching of the mission to the Twelve Apostles (Mk 6:11; Lk 9:5) as a testimony against the people who rejected the call to repentance.

To get to Iconium the apostles probably took the Roman military road, the Via Sebaste which ran through Philomelium (Akşehir) and Laodicea Catacecaumene (Ladik). It was built by the magistrate[10] Cornutus Aquila in 6 BCE and named in honour of Augustus.[11] By the time of Paul's visits the road had become a network connecting the Roman colonies of Pisidia with each other and served as the main artery between the province of Asia and Cilicia and Syria.

Iconium had already a very long history when it was visited by the apostles and was known as Claudiconium after the Roman colony which Claudius had founded by the existing Greek settlement. In Iconium (Konya) 'they entered the Jewish synagogue and spoke in such a way that a great number of both Jews and Greeks came to believe' (Acts 14:1). However, not all the Jews believed and the Christian message gave rise to argument and division in the city, rather than to brotherly love. The apostles' stay in the city was perhaps several months long. Hearing that their adversaries were planning to stone

[10] Latin *propraetor* , the state office next in rank to consulship.

[11] Greek *Sebastos,* 'Augustus' ('Exalted-one').

Frieze piece decorated with garlanded sacrificial bull's head from the imperial temple. Antioch in Pisidia. First half of the first century CE.

them, Paul and his companions fled. Nevertheless, they returned here from Lystra to exhort the faithful, before leaving the region.

Though not specifically mentioned, it is possible that Paul came again to Iconium when passing through Galatia on his second and third journeys. The only other material relating to Paul's stay in Iconium is the story about him and Thecla in the apocryphal Acts of Paul. Later tradition has named the easternmost of the two conical mountain peaks which command the landscape of Iconium to the west after her.[12] The other one is named after Philip who according to one tradition travelled to Hierapolis and Ephesus by way of Iconium.

Fleeing from Iconium, the apostles seem to have found themselves on the road to Lystra which was about a day's walk by the Via Sebaste, some 30 km south. During this period the region where Lystra and Derbe were located was known as Lycaonia. At Lystra there was a crippled man, lame from birth, who had never walked. He listened to Paul speaking, who looked intently at him, saw that he had the faith to be healed, and called out in a loud voice, 'Stand up straight on your feet'. He jumped up and began to walk about.

[12] Today's 'Takkeli Dağ', 'Thecla Mountain'.

When the crowds saw what Paul had done, they cried out in Lycaonian: 'The gods have come down to us in human form'. They called Barnabas 'Zeus' and Paul 'Hermes', because the latter was the chief speaker (Acts 14:8-12).

Obviously the people with whom the apostles first came in contact were the uneducated local population and when Paul healed a cripple they were at first thought to be gods, and the people hailed them in their native tongue as Zeus and Hermes.

In Lystra the crowds' belief that the gods had arrived in their city in the likeness of men was not surprising. In their world gods often made themselves visible, even participated in the banquets prepared in their honour. Early Christian writings mention Barnabas' having a tall and imposing appearance and this must have caused him to be identified with Zeus. Paul, the speaker less significant than his companion, could be Hermes, the god with the gift of eloquence.

The anthropomorphic pagan gods worshipped in the region included Zeus/Jupiter and Hermes/Mercury. The latter, herald and messenger of gods and protector of travellers was a well-known god whose shrines were encountered even between milestones. It is known that in some parts of Anatolia, Zeus was associated with other deities.

Although the very persons whom the apostles encountered at this point may not have known it, Greek mythology associates the region with the visit of Zeus and Hermes during the time of the great flood as told by the Roman poet Ovid in *Metamorphoses* written a few decades before Paul was born:

'Jupiter visited this place, disguised as a mortal, and Mercury, the god who carries the magic wand, laid aside his wings and accompanied his father. The two gods went to a thousand homes, looking for somewhere to rest, and found a thousand homes bolted and barred against them. However, one house took them in: it was, indeed, a humble dwelling roofed with thatch and reeds from the marsh, but a good-hearted old woman, Baucis by name, and her husband Philemon, who was the same age as his wife, had been married in that cottage in their youth, and had grown grey in it together...So, when the heaven-dwellers reached this humble home and, stooping down, entered its low doorway, the old man set chairs for them, and invited them to rest their weary limbs; Baucis bustled up anxiously to throw a rough piece of cloth over the chair, and stirred up the warm ashes on the hearth, fanning the remains of yesterday's fire...Her husband had brought in some vegetables from his

(opposite) Mound of Lystra looking north with the so-called St Paul's spring in the foreground.

carefully-watered garden, and these she stripped of their outer leaves. Philemon took a two-pronged fork and lifted down a side of smoked bacon that was hanging from the blackened rafters; then he cut off a small piece of their long-cherished meat, and boiled it till it was tender in the bubbling water. Meanwhile the old couple chattered on, to pass the time, and kept their guests from noticing the delay. There was a beechwood bowl there, hanging from a nail by its curved handle, which was filled with warm water, and the visitors washed in this, to refresh themselves. On a couch with frame and legs of willow-wood lay a mattress, stuffed with soft sedge grass. Baucis and Philemon covered this with the cloths which they used to put out only on solemn holidays...Then the gods took their places for the meal.'

The meal that the poor couple prepared for the gods included various delicacies. After wiping the table with some stacks of fresh mint, Baucis placed wild cherries, radishes, cheese, eggs roasted in ashes, nuts, figs, dates, plums and wine. When the dinner was over Zeus and Hermes revealed themselves:

''We are gods'', they said, ''and this wicked neighbourhood is going to be punished as it richly deserves; but you will be allowed to escape this disaster. All you have to do is to leave your home, and climb up the steep mountainside with us''. The two old people both did as they were told and, leaning on their sticks, struggled up the long slope. When they were a bowshot distant from the top, they looked round and saw all the rest of their country drowned in marshy waters, only their own home left standing. As they gazed in astonishment, and wept for the fate of their people, their old cottage, which had been small, even for two, was changed into a temple: marble columns took the place of its wooden supports, the thatch grew yellow, till the roof seemed to be made of gold, the doors appeared magnificently adorned with carvings, and marble paved the earthen floor.'

Among the archaeological material which is brought to light in the central Anatolia and related to Hermes or Zeus, the most interesting is a sculpted bust of the latter accompanied by an image of an eagle (Konya Archaeological Museum), his attribute, and Hermes, his travel companion during the terrestrial sojourn in Phrygia.

The news of the wonder worked by the two strangers spread through the streets of Lystra and the priest of the temple of Zeus hurried to find sacrificial bulls bearing garlands. The apostles tore their garments in the customary Jewish reaction against blasphemy and the most common expression of grief

"Men, why are you doing this? We are of the same nature as you, human beings" (Acts 14:15).

Altar stone from Lystra with the name of the city. Second century CE. Konya Archaeological Museum. The inscription in Latin reads: 'Twice fortunate Lystra [Lustra], a Julian colony dedicated [the altar] to the divine Augustus Decreed by the city council'.

in the ancient Near East. In answer to the pagan Lycaonians the apostle, 'Hermes' called upon their experience and knowledge of God, who at last had given a supreme revelation of himself, to turn 'from these idols to the living God', advice which he would later repeat to the philosophers of Athens (Acts 17:24-31).

The events in Lystra give us an idea of how things were in a small Anatolian pagan town at the time of Paul's missionary journeys. The apostles may have encountered many a similar settlement and event during their travels. A similar incident would later happen in Malta where Paul's ship was wrecked during his journey to Rome. Here, when the natives saw a viper hanging from Paul's hand without doing him any harm, they thought that he was a god disguised as a man (Acts 28:3-5). The event also brings to mind the centurion Cornelius' falling at the feet of Peter when he is greeting the latter in a manner appropriate to a deity (Acts 10:25). Both archaeological findings and ancient literature show that if there was one thing that Anatolia of this period was not short of, it was gods and goddesses. This was a period when politics, social and economic life, fortune and the future of people were all integrated into religion. Be it a metropolis like Ephesus or a countryside town like Lystra, sanctuaries and altars of smaller or larger size could be seen everywhere. There were even nameless altars dedicated to 'unknown gods' so that the deities whose worship may have been neglected unknowingly should not be offended.

Acts does not say if the apostles were successful in Lystra. However, at least a family of a grandmother, Lois, mother, Eunice, and son, Timothy accepted the Christian faith (2 Tim 1:5). The grandmother and the mother were Jewesses and the latter had married a Greek. Her son, Timothy, although not circumcised, probably had been raised in the manner of a Jewish youth. He would become a travel companion of Paul during next journey and serve as his secretary.

The place of Lystra (Hatunsaray) has been identified by the discovery of a stone altar, standing in its original site, which gives the name of the site as Lustra. Its inscription indicates the existence of a temple dedicated to Augustus in the city. This may have been the temple of Zeus referred to as being 'at the entrance to the city' (Acts 14:13).

Yet from Lystra too, having preached the gospel, they were expelled, at the behest of a delegation of Jews from Antioch in Pisidia and Iconium. Later in his letters Paul would refer to these events saying 'once I was stoned' (2 Cor 11:25) and also 'persecutions, and sufferings, such as happened to me in

Mound of Derbe looking west.

Antioch, Iconium, and Lystra, persecutions that I endured' (2 Tim 3:11).

Derbe was, however, the only place where the apostles were not persecuted. Acts just mentions that they preached the gospel and made many disciples although only one, Gaius from Derbe (The Western Text says 'Doberus' which would be in Macedonia), one of Paul's companions between Greece and Alexandria Troas during his third journey is mentioned by name (Acts 20:4). Later, when Paul in his letter to the Galatians said 'you did not show disdain or contempt because of the trial caused you by my physical condition, but rather you received me as an angel of the God, and Christ Jesus' (Gal 4:14) he may have been addressing particularly the people of Derbe. Also, later when he refers to the past 'persecutions, and sufferings, such as happened to me in Antioch, Iconium, and Lystra' he does not mention Derbe among these cities.

The site of Derbe (Kerti Höyük) was located a few decades ago owing to an inscription discovered at the site. There is almost nothing known about the

Limestone block with the name of Derbe from the city. Second century CE. Konya Archaeological Museum. The surviving part of the inscription in Greek begins with the seventh line and means 'the gods of Derbe having manifested themselves, the council and people, in the time of Cornelius Dexter, the governor [dedicated this altar].' Sextus Cornelius Dexter is known to have served as the governor in the region in 157 CE.

history of the settlement except the fact that in the first century BCE the town served as headquarters for a notorious tyrant named Antipater until he was killed by the Galatian king Amyntas (37-25 BCE) and that it was also occupied during the Byzantine period.

From Derbe the apostles could have travelled overland to Antioch on the Orontes by way of the Cilician Gates. This might have been more practical than going back through the cities of the furious Jewish communities they had visited or by the deep gorges of the Cestrus river. Also they would have avoided the hot coastal plain unsuitable for the apostle's health.

Paul and Barnabas however, returned by the same way he had travelled before. From Derbe they retraced their steps to Lystra, Iconium, Antioch in Pisidia and Perge. In each of these places they ordained elders or presbyters, whose duties would have consisted of instructing the new converts and baptising children. This shows that, in spite of difficulties, they had made some converts. The early history of the most of these established churches is clouded in darkness.

The visits to these inland cities, with the exception of Antioch in Pisidia, probably incidental. Paul's missionary objective was directed to the well-populated urban centres, often situated on the coast; and thus accessible by the sea. Despite his failure in the region, however, his determination would not permit him to forget the Galatians and he would visit them again and again on both his second and third journeys.

Acts (14:25) informs us that Paul, on his return from this journey from Antioch in Pisidia went to Attaleia after preaching at Perge. The narrator of Acts does not give any information concerning new converts or whether they were persecuted at Perge. It is not known whether Paul's purpose in going Attaleia was to proclaim the gospel there, something he had missed when he first arrived in Pamphylia from Cyprus, or just to find a vessel bound for Seleucia Pieria from where they could easily travel to Antioch on the Orontes. Attaleia was founded by the king Attalus II (159-138 BCE) of Pergamum and at this time was a thriving Roman port. Among the ruins which are visible today there is nothing which dates back to the time of Paul except the ancient harbour which was in use then. As the boat of the apostles slowly moved out of the harbour and the worn out peaks of the Taurus mountains rose in the distance the apostles had covered about 2,000 km, mostly on foot during this first journey.

MINISTRY IN ANTIOCH ON THE ORONTES

The news that Paul had allowed Gentiles into the church was shocking for the Jewish circles of Judea and was met with violent opposition. The latter claimed that the people who did not observe the Jewish dietary obligations and who were not circumcised, could not adhere to Christianity. Thus, in Antioch, a major controversy arose, concerning Jewish purity laws governing food, sharing of meals with Gentiles and circumcision.

One of the practices which separated the Gentile converts from the Jewish Christians was Sabbath, the day of prayer and rest during which the latter withdrew from public life. However, Jewish groups differed about regulations of Sabbath and when Jesus healed the man who was ill for thirty-eighth years at the pool of Bethesda (Jn 5:1-18) he had made the latter carry his bed on the Sabbath. A second distinguishing mark was the food laws commanded for Jewish people. Even if the very complicated prescriptions detailed in the Book of Leviticus may not have been generally practiced in the first-century Jewish world, what was applicable segregated Jews from Gentiles. The main reason why Jews were against sharing meals with Gentiles was the fact that much of the meat which would have been available to the latter at the market came from the sacrifices to pagan gods. Consequently, an invitation to a Gentile dinner always carried the potential danger of eating this meat and compromising, unknowingly, with pagan sacrifice. Some Jewish groups to prevent this danger provided their own food. Although this problem had already found its answer by the visions of the centurion Cornelius and Peter which ended up with Gentiles' receiving the Holy Spirit just as the Jewish Christians (Acts 10) it seems that some Jewish Christians had began avoiding Gentile dinners. In his letter to the Galatians Paul informs us that when they met in Antioch he criticized Peter for stopping sharing food with the Gentiles: 'I said to Kephas[1] in front of all, "If you, though a Jew, are living like a Gentile and not like a Jew, how can you compel the Gentiles to live like Jews?" ' (Gal 2:14). Obviously the practice of Peter would have resulted in two groups of Christians who could not meet for the Eucharist.

Another problem, as important as the dietary laws, was more evident. At the time of Paul, circumcision had been in practice in Africa and although biblical tradition claims it to have been practiced since the patriarch Abraham it may have been first introduced into the Semitic world of Mesopotamia by

(opposite) Grotto-church of St Peter in Antakya.

'Some who had come down from Judea were instructing the brothers, "unless you are circumcised according to the Mosaic practice, you cannot be saved" ' (Acts 15:1).

---

[1] Peter's name in Aramaic. Greek *Petros*, 'rock'.

Jews at the time of the Exodus. It was originally indicated by a tattoo showing that the circumcised person was a member of the tribe.[2] The law of Moses required that all male Jews had to be circumcised in infancy. The obligation had come to be regarded as more important during the later history of the Jewish nation when they lived under the rule of the Babylonians and Persians who did not practice it, and gained a religious meaning. The Jews claimed that all the converts to Christianity had also to be circumcised. The Old Testament refers to the employment of primitive flint knives for the operation. At that time it was also a dangerous and painful operation especially for adults.

It was decided that Paul and Barnabas taking Titus with them should go to Jerusalem, to discuss such matters with the elders and apostles there. In Jerusalem after much discussion, it was decided that as long as Gentiles did not eat meat sacrificed to the idols and blood-meat and avoided marriage within forbidden degrees of affinity, there was nothing to prevent them from becoming Christians. Thus the complex obligations of the Jewish law had been reduced to a few prohibitions. Although in the conclusion summarized by James the Just (Acts 15) there is no word about circumcision, and other obligations such as the eating of pig or sabbath, one may conclude that they were abrogated as well. It is known that with the resolution of these matters pagans did not flee to baptism, but their cancellation would ultimately determine the character of the doctrine and practices of Christianity and help its spread.

The Apostolic Council held in Jerusalem also decided that Paul should continue to preach to the Gentiles and James the Just, Peter and John to the Jews (Gal 2:2-10). Paul's fluent Greek may have been one of the reasons why he was chosen to preach to the Gentiles and hellenized Jews.

Following the meeting Judas, who was called Barsabbas, and Silas (also called Silvanus) were chosen to accompany the apostles to Antioch with a letter to the Gentiles in Antioch, Syria and Cilicia stating that Barnabas and Paul had been chosen, together with Judas and Silas, to take the message that they were required only to abstain from meat sacrificed to idols, from meats of strangled animals, also from blood in any flesh, and from unlawful marriage.

[2] The wedding ring, according to some scholars, originated from the practice of wearing the cut foreskin, later to be replaced by a ring.

(opposite) Biblical inscription. The mosaic was found in Antioch on the Orontes and dates from the first half of the fifth century. Hatay Archaeological Museum. Antakya. In Greek the inscription reads: 'Peace be your coming in, you who gaze on this. Joy and blessing be those who stay here. The mosaic floor of the triclinium was made in the time of Megas and Ioannes and Anthousa, 'stathmouchoi', in the month of Gorpiaios, in the fifth indiction'. The mosaic probably belonged to an inn and the term 'stathmochos' means innkeeper. The first words of the inscription are encountered in 1 Samuel 16:4 as 'is your visit peaceful, O seer?', addressed by the elders of Bethlehem to Samuel when he entered the town.

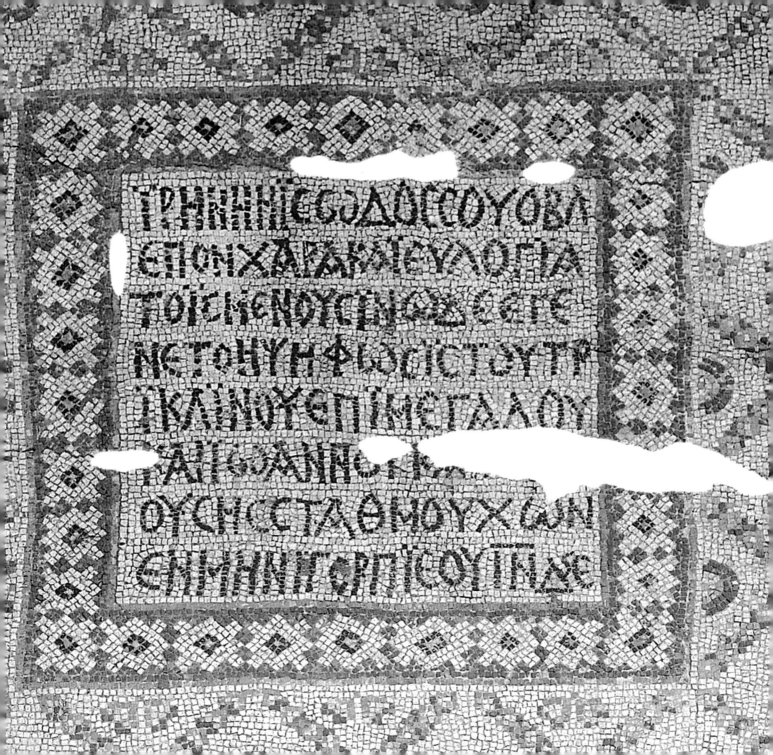

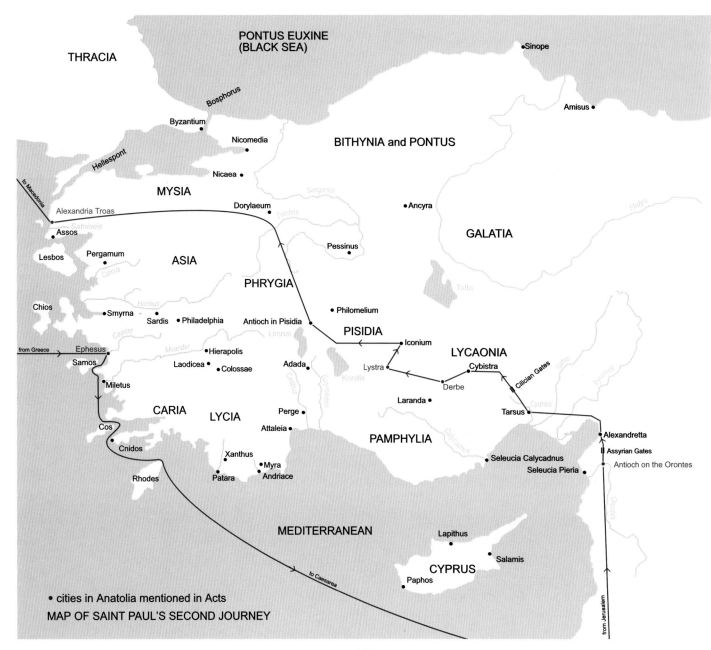

THRACIA

PONTUS EUXINE
(BLACK SEA)

•Sinope

Amisus •

Bosphorus

Byzantium

Nicomedia

BITHYNIA and PONTUS

Hellespont

Nicaea •

to Macedonia

MYSIA

Dorylaeum

Sangarius

Alexandria Troas

Tembris

Ancyra

Satnioeis

Assos

Pessinus

GALATIA

Lesbos

Pergamum

ASIA

PHRYGIA

Halys

Chios

Hermus

Smyrna

Sardis

• Philadelphia

Philomelium

Tatta

Antioch in Pisidia

PISIDIA

Iconium

LYCAONIA

from Greece

Ephesus

Cayster

Meander

Hierapolis

Limnai

Lystra

Cybistra

Saros

Samos

Laodicea

• Colossae

Adada

Derbe

Cilician Gates

Miletus

Cayster

Koralis

Laranda •

Tarsus

Pyramus

CARIA

LYCIA

Perge

Cos

Caestus

Eurymedon

Attaleia

PAMPHYLIA

Cydnus

Cnidos

Alexandretta

Xanthus

Assyrian Gates

Rhodes

Myra

Seleucia Calycadnus

Antioch on the Orontes

Patara

Andriace

Seleucia Pieria

MEDITERRANEAN

Lapithus

Orontes

CYPRUS

Salamis

to Caesarea

Paphos

from Jerusalem

• cities in Anatolia mentioned in Acts

MAP OF SAINT PAUL'S SECOND JOURNEY

PAUL'S SECOND JOURNEY

Antioch on the Orontes — Derbe — Lystra — Iconium — Antioch in Pisidia — Alexandria Troas — Neapolis — Philippi — Thessalonica — Beroea — Athens — Corinth — **Ephesus** — Caesarea — **Antioch on the Orontes**

After a few years, the Gentile mission now accepted, the elders in Antioch and Jerusalem decided for a second journey. This time Paul and Barnabas went their separate ways, ostensibly because they disagreed over the suitability of John Mark, but perhaps also because of Paul's more radical views as to the rights of Gentiles. At this date Paul had not yet forgiven Mark's desertion in Perge. Whilst Barnabas and John Mark went to Cyprus, Paul left Antioch perhaps in the spring of 49, accompanied by Silas and began a second missionary journey. The latter's being a Roman citizen was also an advantage.

The preaching of the gospel at Ephesus, the rich cosmopolitan metropolis of the Roman province of Asia, was probably the major objective of this journey. Paul also wanted to check how his first converts in the churches of Galatia were doing. Recently, he had heard of their apostasy and was probably compelled to write them (p 110).

There was only one overland route to Galatia. This had been in use centuries before Paul's time and is still in use today. After they left Antioch, the apostles probably skirted the Amuq (Amık) plain until they reached the Amanus mountain, the southernmost extension of the Taurus chain. They must have crossed the Amanus by the Assyrian Gates[1] and descended to the Mediterranean coast, to Alexandretta ad Issum (İskenderun), another city founded by Alexander the Great, and passing by the battleground of Issus (333 BCE) continued towards Cilicia. The name of this fertile plain is thought to have derived from its name when it was a part of the Assyrian 'Khilakku' domain and later the satrapy of Hlk=Hilik established here by the Persians. It

'After some time, Paul said to Barnabas, "Come, let us make a return visit to see how the brothers are getting on in all the cities where we proclaimed the word of the Lord" ' (Acts 15:36).

[1] Also known as the Syrian Gates. Today's 'Belen' Pass.

was fed by the rivers Pyramus (Ceyhan) and Sarus (Seyhan). In antiquity, like that of the river Cestrus of Perge, the deltas created by these rivers were infected with malaria. From Antioch on the Orontes it would have taken a walk of a week to reach Tarsus. It is very probable that Paul visited his Christian friends before departure, and they refreshed their supplies for the long trip awaiting them. The shortest connection between the southern plain and inland Anatolia was established by the Cilician Gates (Gülek Boğazı) which was a narrow pass of 3 m width. The pass was the gate to central Anatolia and had been carefully guarded even by the ancient kingdoms which ruled in the region. During the late Hittite period it was known as Mt Muti. Crossing it in 401 BCE, Xenophon in *Anabasis* describes it as having 'consisted of a carriage track which was tremendously steep; impassable for any army if there was any opposition'. The Cilician Gates was supplanted by a number of difficult passes and despite the existence of the Roman road which transversed them going through these gorges was a difficult part of Paul's journeys. Writing in 50 CE when he served as the governor of Cilicia, the Roman statesman Cicero says 'Snow makes the Taurus impassable before June', a statement probably concerning Roman troops and baggage trains rather than individual travellers.

Shortly after crossing the Cilician Gates the landscape changed. This was the beginning of central Anatolia which was a dry, vast, high plateau known at the time of Paul as Galatia. Research has shown that it was once, some ten or fifteen millennia before, occupied by an inland sea. The present day Salt lake (Tuz gölü) known at that time as lake Tatta is what is left of it. Where water supplies permitted it could give adequate grain harvests, but much of it was a dusty dun-coloured expanse which became a barren waste at the centre. Since their invitation by the king Nicomedes I of Bithynia to serve as mercenaries around 287 BCE, the region had become the home of Celtic tribes or Gauls, and was named Galatia. Originally forming a military aristocracy, the Gauls remained a minority of a population that was largely native Phrygian and Cappadocian.

The southern province of Galatia at the time of Paul's journeys, was known as Lycaonia. It was a largely pastoral area, with large flocks of sheep and goats and other animals, even wild asses. Water lies in some 50 m depth. The journey of Cyrus the Younger and his army through this area may be regarded as the earliest contact of the native population with Greek culture. Although the region would be subdued by general Perdikkas of Alexander

(opposite) A stretch of the Roman road, leading from Tarsus to the Cilician Gates and beyond. During the Roman era the 'East Road' from Syria and the 'West Road' from Anchiale (Mersin ?) met near Tarsus and continued to inland Anatolia by the Cilician Gates. The road is paved with well-fitted limestone blocks secured by curbstones. An inscription in Latin carved into the rocks to the southwestern end of the surviving part of the road mentions Marcus Aurelius (161-80 CE) who probably built or repaired it. The triumphal arch in the picture may have also belonged to him.

the Great, the actual penetration of the Greek language and culture had to wait for the establishment of the Roman colonies shortly before Paul's visits. When Paul came this way, many people spoke their own language, although as elsewhere, Greek was the common language. Even though a network of Roman roads traversed it, the region remained remote, and its few cities were situated along the highway. It is very probable that until he reached Antioch in Pisidia Paul followed the western branch of the main Roman thoroughfare known as the Cilician road. Coming out of the Taurus range this artery turned west and by way of Cybistra (Ereğli) reached Derbe. Thus, following the first mission's route in the opposite direction from Derbe the apostle continued to Lystra probably by way of Laranda (Karaman), Iconium and Antioch in Pisidia. Except for Lystra the activities of the apostle during his second missionary journey through this region are not known. However, Paul would not have missed visiting his acquaintances in these churches.

Although he had been stoned at Lystra this had taken place about a year ago and by this time the magistrates in the city were expected to have changed. Here Paul was joined by a young disciple, Timothy, whose father was Gentile, but whose mother was a Jewish convert to Christianity. In spite of Paul's belief that circumcision was not necessary for salvation, a fact which was officially established by the Apostolic Council, for expedience he had Timothy circumcised (Acts 16:3). Although his behaviour seems to contradict his words 'if you have yourselves circumcised, Christ will be of no benefit to you' (Gal 5:2), as a practical man Paul might have wanted to avoid unforeseen problems when preaching to Jewish communities.

After a trip through the cities of southern Galatia and Pisidia in the spring the prospect of going to Ephesus, a city with a coastal swamp for a harbour, may not have looked attractive. He was prevented from going into the province of Asia by the Holy Spirit. The hills around Antioch in Pisidia were the western extremity of the Phrygian plateau. From Pisidia, Paul, Silas and Timothy must have avoided the dry central plateau and travelled through the Phrygian highlands which were never short of sweet water springs and towns established in the pockets of the mountains. The Royal Road which Herodotus claims to have been built by Darius I (522-486 BCE) and connected Sardis to Susa also ran through this region. To reach Ephesus the shortest and easiest route at the time that the apostle and his friends hit this ancient highway was to follow it to the

'On account of the Jews of that region, Paul had him circumcised, for they all knew that his father was a Greek' (Acts 16:3).

west. If they had continued on it to the end it would have taken them through the Hermus valley to Sardis. They, however, seem to have crossed the highway somewhere and travelled northwest towards Dorylaeum (Eskişehir).

Somewhere between Mysia and Bithynia Paul had a vision, which prevented him continuing in this direction. If Paul had continued in this direction, he would have reached the populated cities of Prusa (Bursa), Nicaea (İznik) and Nicomedia (İzmit) and finally Byzantium. The prospect of preaching the gospel in the populated urban centres across the Aegean, and even eventually further west at Rome, was always in the apostle's mind. They travelled west, to the Aegean coast whose harbours were never short of vessels to the islands and Macedonia. Troas, also known as Troad, was the name of the northwestern projection of Anatolia into the Aegean. It extended north from Adramyttium (Edremit) to the Hellespont (Dardanelles). Its highest point was Mt Ida (Kaz Dağı, 1767 m) where Paris once acted as the arbitrator for the beauty contest which is said, ultimately, to have led to the Trojan war. The major cities of the region were Assos, Troia and Alexandria Troas.

In Alexandria Troas the apostle saw another vision, very probably an allusion to Luke, telling him to go to Macedonia. The first encounter of Luke, the narrator of 'We-sections' in Acts,[2] and Paul is thought to have taken place here. This meeting was very probably accidental because until he reached the border of Mysia and Bithynia, the apostle had not yet decided which way to travel. Luke was a Greek physician, the 'beloved physician' (Col 4:14), and according to one tradition 'by birth' from Antioch on the Orontes, a hypothesis originating from the detailed manner in which he recounts the development of Christianity in that city. He might have also met Paul there. His parents are thought to have obtained Roman citizenship when Julius Caesar gave it to the physicians in Rome. A second tradition claims that he was a native of Macedonia whom Paul met in Alexandria Troas and converted. It has been suggested that the party, now of four, decided to cross to Macedonia on the initiative of Luke who was familiar with the region.

Although Luke begins narrating the events as a member of the group it is difficult to know exactly if he simply used 'we', first person plural, as a literary device to colour the incidents. The realistic way that the events are recounted

'A Macedonian stood before him and implored him with these words, "Come over to Macedonia and help us" ' (Acts 16:9).

[2] The other 'We-sections' are (Acts 16:10-18; 20:5-16; 21:1-18; 27:28-29).

after this point give the impression that even if he was not there during the 'we' events, he may have used another eyewitness' story. Acts does not mention any ministry in the city during this first visit to Alexandria Troas. The apostle would visit the city during his next journey and preach the gospel.

Alexandria Troas was founded around 310 BCE by Antigonus I, a general of Alexander who had inherited the European portion of the hero's empire after his death, and named it Antigonia. After defeating Antigonus at Ipsus (301 BCE), the victor, Lysimachus (another general of Alexander) renamed the city in honour of Alexander and added the word 'Troas' to distinguish it from Alexandria in Egypt. It was strategically situated on sea and land routes and had later become a Roman colony. With its small but well-protected harbour, which is still very impressive the city was then a major trading post. The warm springs of the region still attract many visitors as in the past. All that can be seen of this large and overgrown site are some remains of the baths built by Herodes Atticus in the first half of the following century.

From Alexandria Troas Paul and his friends took a boat to the island of Samothrace to continue their journey towards Macedonia; Neapolis (Kavala) and further to Philippi. His meeting there with Lydia, a citizen of Thyateira, a dealer in purple cloth, is interesting in showing the lively commercial world of this period in the Aegean.

After eighteen months of labour in Macedonia and Greece, Paul and his fellow tentmakers, Aquila and Priscilla, departed from Cenchreae, the eastern harbour of Corinth, for Ephesus. Aquila was a Jew, originally from the Roman province of Pontus, and with his wife Priscilla, had settled in Rome. They were among the Jewish population that the emperor Claudius had banished from Rome (Acts 18:2) and were already Christians when Paul met them in Corinth. The Roman historian Suetonius, who was born shortly after Paul's martyrdom, informs us that 'Because the Jews at Rome caused continuous disturbances at the instigation of Chrestus he expelled them from the city'.

The historian's reference is short and it is not clear if he means Christ or any other Jesus movement unknown to us. If he means Christ, it is the earliest reference of its kind outside Christian literature. It may be that some Jewish Christians who regarded Jesus as the expected messiah[3] may have been

(opposite) Ancient harbour of Alexandria Troas which Paul visited several times. Beyond the Aegean is Tenedos (Bozcaada).

[3] Hebrew *Mashiah*, 'Anointed One'; Greek *Christos*.

opposed by other Jews. Claudius seems, despite his lenient rule, and tolerance for Jews to have followed the characteristic Roman attitude at the time of disturbances and punished all of the insurgents by expulsion.

It was after this event that Aquila and Priscilla (a diminutive of the Roman name Prisca) arrived in Corinth where they met Paul. The couple may have accompanied Paul to Ephesus, in addition to their religious enthusiasm, to find more profitable business opportunities, for the city was famous for the manufacture of tents and marquees. This was a period when people travelled safely and easily from one place to the other for different purposes. It is also suggested that towards the end of his second journey Paul's health was not good and the couple accompanied him as far as Ephesus. This may account for the fast trip of the apostle from Corinth to Antioch on the Orontes by way of Ephesus.

It is also probable that Aquila and Priscilla went to Ephesus and stayed there to make preparations for Paul's third journey; because, eventually, one of the congregations in Ephesus met in their house (Rom 16:5). This unusual couple were deeply committed to their religion. The apostle admits that at least once they 'risked their necks' for his life (Rom 16:3-4).

The writer of Acts says that before sailing from Greece Paul 'had his hair cut because he had taken a vow' (Acts 18:18). The reason for undertaking this Nazirite vow is not known. The apostle may have wanted to demonstrate his Jewish origins to the Corinthian Jews. Or he may have been sick. According to the Jewish custom one did this when one was ill, or in distress and followed the observances elaborated in the Book of Numbers (6).[4] To unbind the vow he would shave his head and keep his hair to be burned as a sacrifice at the altar of the Jerusalem Temple. Since the Corinthian mission had been successful and there was no reason to be distressed, the vow Paul had taken is thought to have concerned his sickness at Corinth, another place infected with malaria. Later in his letter to the Romans — in the last part claimed to have been addressed to the Ephesians — when he introduces Phoebe of Corinth saying 'she has been a benefactor to many and to me as well' (Rom 16:1) he may have been referring to his sickness there and Phoebe's nursing of him. Luke should certainly have known of the apostle's illness; but as a discreet physician

---

[4] Also Acts 21:23-24.

faithful to his Hippocratic oath, does not give any information about it.

At the time that the apostle's boat arrived, Ephesus was on the sea with its port at the mouth of the Cayster river (Küçük Menderes). Strabo, writing some forty years before the arrival of Paul, says that the harbour was already silted up. Almost none of the monuments whose ruins are visible today was yet built when Paul visited Ephesus. In addition to this the great earthquake of 17 CE had destroyed what was left from its previous Hellenistic history.

During his short stay Paul must have visited the local synagogue, probably on the Sabbath when the people were assembled. The place where the synagogue of Ephesus stood is not known. But the departure of his ship prevented him from staying longer. The reason may have been that the sea voyage which awaited him was long and it was already autumn, the end of the sailing season in 52.

Aquila and Priscilla remained in Ephesus where they became prominent figures of the Christian community. During the absence of the apostle, Apollos, an Alexandrian Jew, who was well-read in the Old Testament and a good speaker came to the city. It is difficult to understand if Apollos was a Christian, and if so, where he had been 'instructed in the way of the Lord'. He 'spoke and thought accurately about Jesus' but had not received baptism. The 'baptism of John' stands for 'baptism with water' as a symbol of repentance but not baptism in the name of Jesus.

The information given by Acts leads one to think that Apollos was preaching 'a Baptist sect' which perhaps existed separately, even in competition with the Christian church. Priscilla and Aquila, who had listened to him speak in the Ephesian synagogue, were impressed but also concerned about his lack of understanding of the power of the Holy Spirit, so they 'took him aside and explained to him the way [of God] more accurately. And when he wanted to cross Achaia, the brothers encouraged him and wrote to the disciples to welcome him.'

The story of Apollos shows that in addition to Paul, there were other Christian preachers who frequented the metropolises of the Greco-Roman world whether they were authorized or not.

Thus, from Ephesus Paul took the ship to Caesarea from where he travelled to Antioch on the Orontes by land.

"I shall come back to you again, God willing" (Acts 18:21).

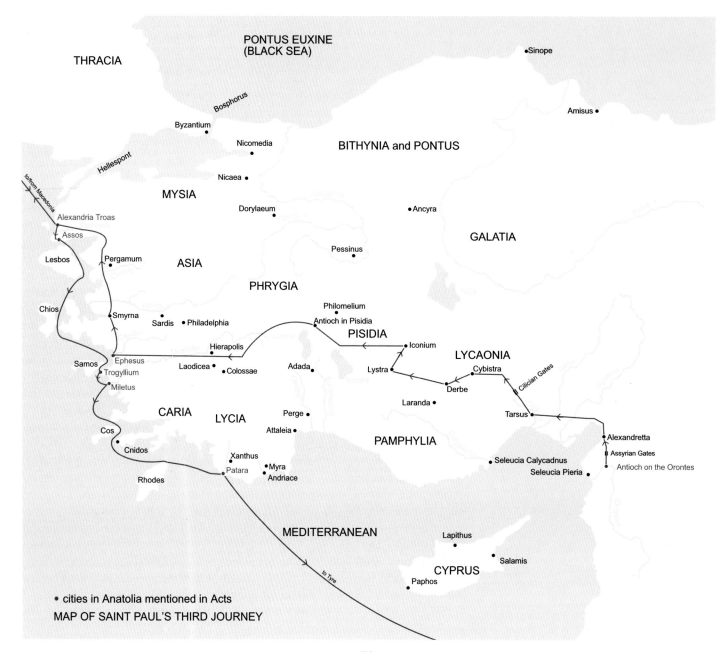

MAP OF SAINT PAUL'S THIRD JOURNEY

THRACIA

PONTUS EUXINE
(BLACK SEA)

• Sinope

Bosphorus

• Amisus

Byzantium •

Nicomedia •

BITHYNIA and PONTUS

Hellespont

to/from Macedonia

Nicaea •

MYSIA

Dorylaeum •

• Ancyra

Alexandria Troas

GALATIA

Assos •

Pessinus •

Lesbos

Pergamum •

ASIA

Chios

PHRYGIA

Philomelium •

Smyrna •

Antioch in Pisidia

Sardis • • Philadelphia

PISIDIA

Iconium •

LYCAONIA

Hierapolis •

Ephesus

Laodicea •

• Colossae

Adada •

Lystra •

Cybistra •

Samos

Derbe •

Cilician Gates

Trogyllium •

Laranda •

Tarsus •

• Miletus

CARIA

LYCIA

Perge •

Cos •

Attaleia •

PAMPHYLIA

Alexandretta •

Cnidos •

Xanthus •

Assyrian Gates

Rhodes

Patara

• Myra

Andriace •

Seleucia Calycadnus •

Antioch on the Orontes

Seleucia Pieria •

MEDITERRANEAN

Lapithus •

to Tyre

CYPRUS

Salamis •

Paphos •

• cities in Anatolia mentioned in Acts
MAP OF SAINT PAUL'S THIRD JOURNEY

PAUL'S THIRD JOURNEY

Antioch on the Orontes — Derbe — Lystra — Iconium — Antioch in Pisidia — Ephesus — Alexandria Troas — Corinth — Philippi — Thessalonica — Beroea — **Alexandria Troas — Assos —** Lesbos — Chios — Samos — **Trogyllium — Miletus —** Cos — Rhodes — **Patara** — Tyre — Ptolemais — Caesarea — Jerusalem

After a short stay in Antioch, in the spring of 53 Paul set out on his third missionary journey. This time the main objective of his mission was again Ephesus, the largest city of the Roman province of Asia, to which the Holy Spirit had allowed him to go and preach but briefly during his previous journey. As he had done before, eager to visit the congregations in Galatia, Paul preferred to travel overland, most probably by the route of his previous journey: by way of the Assyrian Gates, Tarsus, and the Cilician Gates into Lycaonia. It is very probable that he visited Derbe, Lystra, Iconium and Antioch in Pisidia to see how the nucleus of the Christian community at each of these cities was doing. Acts informs us that after this point Paul 'travelled through the interior of the country' (Acts 19:1) and arrived at Ephesus where he is said to have remained for almost three years. From the Lycus valley if he followed the Roman roads of the time he would have travelled through the 'interior of the country' either by way of the Meander valley to Ephesus or through Philadelphia (Alaşehir), Sardis and Smyrna (İzmir) to Ephesus.

When, later, the apostle referred to Asia in his letters (1 Cor 16:19; 2 Cor 1:8), his readers would have understood that this was the large province on the west of Anatolia. At this time, it included the whole of the Aegean coast from Caria, through ancient Ionia and Aeolis to the southern shore of the sea of Marmara, a little to the east of Cyzicus. It embraced Troas, Mysia, Phrygia and Lydia and extended inland through the valleys and headwaters of the Hermus (Gediz) and Maeander (Büyük Menderes) rivers towards the central plateau and the eastern boundary with Galatia. It was the oldest and wealthiest of the Roman provinces of Anatolia and it contained several ancient and famous cities, including Miletus and Smyrna on the coast and inland, the old Lydian capital, Sardis; further north was Pergamum, the wealthy former capital of the Attalids. It was the last king of Pergamum Attalos III who, lacking a

"We have never even heard that there is a holy Spirit" (Acts 19:2).

legitimate heir, had bequeathed his kingdom to Roman people upon his death in 133 BCE. But the greatest of all was Ephesus, the splendid capital and cult centre of Artemis.

The good climate and soil gave rich harvests and much of Asia was well-settled, particularly in the Maeander valley, where Paul would have known some people. The roads which ran along the river beds enabled the rural population to find a market for their agricultural produce in large coastal cities and the Aegean world beyond.

In antiquity, the easiest and safest route from Galatia to the Aegean coast followed the path of the Meander river. To reach this popular road the apostle may have travelled by way of Apamea (Dinar), which had the largest Jewish community in the region, and Laodicea on the Lycus river (Eskihisar). Even if there were some Jewish people in Anatolia as early as the sixth century BCE, their number did not reach substantial figures until the reign of the Seleucid king Antiochus III (223-187 BCE) when he moved two thousand families from Babylonia and Mesopotamia to the fortresses in western Anatolia. These new settlers were given vineyards and grain fields, economic privileges and were allowed to establish separate groups from the natives whom he did not trust for the fact that they had recently supported his uncle who had rebelled against him. They were the descendants of the Ten Tribes which were originally moved to Mesopotamia from Jerusalem in 597 and 586 BCE by the king of Babylon, Nebuchadnezzar, and were claimed to be separated from their brothers by 'the baths and the wines', that is by the luxuries of the Roman way of life according to the later Jewish literature. It seems that these Jewish communities survived into Paul's time because most of the Roman edicts which confirm the privileges such as the freedom of sending money to the Jerusalem Temple, exemption from military service and freedom of worship, come from this region.

When he arrived in Ephesus Paul's friends of the previous mission, Aquila and Priscilla, must have met and informed him about the work of Apollos and the followers of John the Baptizer. Paul had 'found some disciples' but they had never heard of a 'holy Spirit' and were baptised only with the baptism of John. Paul saw that these were rebaptized in the name of the Lord Jesus.

(opposite) Reused Roman sarcophagus lid bearing a menorah and inscription in Greek, which reads 'Belonging to the Jews', at the western necropolis of Hierapolis (Pamukkale).

In the autumn of 54 Paul returned to the synagogue where he had preached during his previous short visit of three years earlier. He spoke of the Kingdom of God. The idea of a messianic Kingdom was familiar to the Jewish listeners since their childhood and for many generations they had been waiting for this. But Paul was saying that it was through Jesus, the true Christ, a man who was crucifiuld together with two thieves sometime ago that this Kingdom was to be ushered in and established. As elsewhere his teaching in the synagogue seems to have lasted only three months. Many of the Jews rejected his teachings.

For the next two years he preached the gospel in the school of Tyrannus who may have rented his halls to visiting lecturers. To strangers the apostle would have appeared as one of the numerous philosophers who travelled from one city to another sharing his knowledge and ideas.

As did other artisans in the city, Paul probably began his daily task as a tentmaker before sunrise and continued until closing time at 11 am as is clearly told in the Western Text. In his speech to the Ephesian elders he reminded them that his hands served both his needs and his companions. Until about 4 pm when most of the artisans began to work again he would have been free to devote himself to the missionary work which was the objective of his stay in the city.

A story in Acts includes the apostle's dealings with the exorcists of Ephesus. Paul's miraculous powers were already well-known. In Lystra he had healed a cripple, in Philippi he had exorcised a slave girl with a spirit of divination, in Malta he would later heal the father of Publius, the chief man of the island, of fever and dysentery (Acts 28:7-8). He continued these practices in Ephesus, to the extent that the faithful touched their handkerchiefs or aprons to the apostle and then carried them to the sick, crediting the clothes with miraculous healing power.

Sarcophagus fragment which comes from the foot of the hill on which so-called St Paul's Prison stands. Second century CE. İstanbul Archaeological Museums. It is decorated with scenes of a sculpture workshop and a race in the gymnasium (a trainer of the three nude boys), a dog and a Herm.

The fame of Ephesus in charm and magic preceded that of the other cities in the empire. Its cosmopolitan rich atmosphere attracted soothsayers, purveyors of charms, magicians or other people of similar tasks from the distant corners of the empire. Exorcising spirits in the name of Jesus was widely practiced in the early church, but the attempt by itinerant Jewish exorcists to do so was clearly usurpation of authority. Their attempt did not succeed, however, and they themselves were overpowered by the evil spirit they sought to control. The point of this story was intended for all Christians; that healings and exorcisms depended as much upon the integrity of the healer as upon the faith of the afflicted. As a result of this incident, some Ephesian practitioners of magic collected and burned their books, said to have been worth 'fifty thousand silver pieces'.

During the time of Paul's missionary works Christian congregations of smaller or larger sizes are thought to have been established at Colossae (Col 1:1) and Hierapolis (Col 4:13) and at the seven cities of the Revelation: Ephesus, Smyrna, Pergamum, Thyateira, Sardis, Philadelphia and Laodicea. Whether Paul visited all of these cities is not known. Groups of believers from the country around Ephesus, however, may have come to listen to his preaching and invite him to their cities for short stays. He had probably visited and met fellow Christians at some of these cities as he travelled from Antioch in Pisidia to Ephesus. The leader of the Christian community in Colossae was Epaphras 'our beloved fellow slave' (Col 1:7). He had been active in the evangelization of two other cities of the Lycus valley, Hierapolis and Laodicea (Col 4:13). Later, while imprisoned — in Ephesus or Rome or Caesarea — Paul addressed a circular letter to the Colossians which they were to share with the Christians in Laodicea. The church in Laodicea met in the house of Nympha (Col 4:15) just as in Ephesus the church met in the house of Aquila and Priscilla (1 Cor 16:19; Rom 16:5), and in Corinth in the house of Gaius (Rom 16:23).

Although Acts does not mention it, the apostle might have been imprisoned during his stay in Ephesus. In his letters to the churches in Greece, Macedonia and Asia he repeatedly refers to his sufferings. If this bondage took place in Ephesus, the charge which led to his imprisonment is not known. It has been suggested that the Ephesian Jews may have built up a case against the apostle, charging him with diverting sums of money which had been collected from the churches he knew, as a relief fund for Jerusalem and which he was carrying with him and that normally would have been sent to its destination. The Jews may have approached the Roman governor, and persuaded him to imprison Paul.

Writing to the church in Corinth from Ephesus, Paul says 'We do not want you to be unaware, brothers, of the affliction that came to us in the province of Asia; we were utterly weighed down beyond our strength, so that we despaired even of life. Indeed, we had accepted within ourselves the sentence of death' (2 Cor 1:8-9), and on another ocasion he refers to his fighting, so to speak, with beasts at Ephesus (1 Cor 15:32). In the Roman world of the period there were only two ways that a person would have fought wild animals. One was to be exposed to them in the arena, in which case, except miraculously, survivals are unknown or by becoming a professional beast-fighter, *bestiarius,* which was out of question in Paul's a case. It is very probable that, when he wrote the sentence, he imagined himself as a fighter of this kind struggling not in flesh but spiritually against the wickedness in Ephesus. The apocryphal Acts of Paul dwells on the apostle's imprisonment in the city. Here, the Ephesians became angry at Paul's speech and imprisoned him until he would be thrown to the lions. Eubola and Artemilla, wives of eminent Ephesian men, visited Paul in the prison at night 'desiring the grace of divine washing'. The apostle took them to the Aegean shore and baptized them. The naming of the watch-tower, which was once the closest to the sea, in the Hellenistic walls of Ephesus as 'St Paul's prison' may have been inspired by this event. Also in his apocryphal Acts, Paul was put into the stadium and a huge lion was let loose on him. But the beast lay down at his feet. The other animals which followed the lion also did not touch the apostle who stood like a statue in prayer. Then a hailstorm poured down killing the other wild animals, saved the lion which escaped to the mountains. The hailstorm also killed some men and sheared off the governor's ear. Seeing what happened he accepted Christianity and was baptized.

Paul had planned to stay in Ephesus until the feast of Pentecost saying 'because a door has opened to me wide, and productive for work' (1 Cor 16:8-9). Some scholars think that this wide-opened door was occasioned by the annual festival of Artemis which provided a splendid opportunity to do

(opposite) Ruins of the Hellenistic tower known as St Paul's prison probably since the seventeenth century. This is the westernmost point of the fortifications built by Lysimachus (306-281 BCE), founder of Ephesus on Mt Coressus (Bülbül Dağı). It is divided into rooms and was probably of two storeys. It is also known as 'Astyagou Pagos', the Hill of Astyages after an inscription in the tower.

Marble votive stele from Sardis. About 400 BCE. Manisa Archaeological Museum. This relief is found at the ancient Lydian capital Sardis and shows that at that time the two goddesses were worshipped separately. They are represented with their attribute animals, Artemis a hind and Cybele a lion. They are dressed in veils and long sleeved chiton-himation costumes. Each one wears a cylindrical *polos*, Anatolian crown. Cybele's tympanum hangs in the upper right corner. On the same side are two worshipers.

missionary work, for during it the city was crowded with people from all over Anatolia, the islands and Greece. In the great Aegean coastal city of Ephesus a truly syncretistic goddess had for centuries attracted her devotees. Here the Anatolian fertility and earth mother goddess had been identified with their own goddess Artemis by the Greek settlers a thousand or so years earlier. The festival was held during the month of Artemision which fell sometime in April or May approximately to the Pentecost.

Though the Greek Artemis (the Roman Diana), a goddess of chastity, the hunt and associated with animals, would seem to bear little resemblance to a fecund earth mother deity, she was a nature goddess and often in her representations, flanked by animals. Moreover, the temples of Artemis, like those of the goddess who preceded her, are always aligned to the west, rather than as with other gods, to the east. The statues of Ephesian Artemis are perhaps the most visible evidence of the syncretistic tendency of ancient religions and of the tolerance, indeed courtesy extended to the gods of others, from whom elements, or indeed the entire deity, might be adopted. With the influence of Greek art, by Paul's time, her figure had lost its large buttocks and big breasts, the symbols of fertility, and was on the way to assuming the slender shape of a Greek goddess. The most prominent feature of her image were the ovals covering her upper body from waist to neck. These are thought to have represented the balls of bulls sacrificed for her during cultic ceremonies and nailed to a wooden statue of the goddess.

The temple of Artemis, the Artemision, which stood in its own precinct outside the city, to which it was joined by a processional way, was regarded as one of the seven wonders of the world in Hellenistic times, on account of its beauty and vast size. The cult statue stood in her shrine, in a long, narrow hall surrounded by 127 columns, forming a veritable forest of marble. The temple also offered sanctuary to criminals such as runaway slaves. It is not known if Onesimus, the slave from Colossae, when he sought Paul in Ephesus (Phlm 10), had originally come to the city to shelter in Artemis' temple. Except for the opportunities it offered as a refuge, the city is situated too close to Colossae for a runaway slave.

As Demetrius, president of the silversmiths' guild claimed (Acts 19:27)

Artemis, worshipped throughout Asia, was supported by the number of pilgrims who attended her festival. She brought great wealth to the city, not only through the sale of votives and various offerings, but because of the large numbers of people who came to her various celebrations and festivals. They had to be fed, lodged, entertained and generally looked after. There was extra work and extra money for everyone, be they jewellers, bakers, washerwomen, fishmongers, shoemakers, musicians, prostitutes, doctors or even lawyers. Festivals then, as now, were big business, producing revenue for the city that held them. But more than that, the city, namely its citizens, gained esteem and lustre and no city in Anatolia was more esteemed or illustrious than Ephesus.

Paul's influence aroused the enmity of the guild of silversmiths who made miniature shrines and offerings for dedication to Artemis. An inscription[1] which dates some forty years after the riot mentions a single offering of 29 images, probably similar to those of Demetrius and his fellow craftsmen. Made of gold and silver and weighing from 1.5 to 4 kg each, they were figures of the goddess with two stags and a variety of smybolic figures. These objects dedicated to Artemis, were carried in public processions throughout the city, and then placed in her temple.

Instigated by Demetrius, president of the guild, a riot broke out. Paul's preaching obviously was threatening their trade. After Demetrius had called together the members of the guild and spoken to them about the economic consequences of Paul's teaching, they angrily rushed forth into the street. Their momentum drew other people most of whom were ignorant of what was going on. On their way to the theatre they seized the apostle's companions, Gaius and Aristarchus of Macedonia.

The scene of the riot was the Hellenistic theatre of Ephesus which was then being enlarged with the addition of new seats for spectators and a stage building. The Jews put forward a man named Alexander to address the mob, probably because they feared that the crowd might turn against them for their own hostility to images. The crowd refused to hear him and for about two hours shouted 'Great is Artemis of the Ephesians!'.

[1] Discovered in the theatre and moved to the nearby lower agora.

Relief with prisoners and their guard from Miletus. Second-third centuries CE. İstanbul Archaeological Museums. A group of condemned probably being led to the circus by their custodian. The prisoners are clad in loincloths and bound by a rope by their necks from their shackles.

The 'clerk of the people' finally managed to calm the crowd. After all the most important of his responsibilities was avoiding disturbances of any kind in the city. He told them that the supremacy of Artemis was not in peril, that the Christians had neither robbed the temple nor blasphemed her, and everybody knew that her statue had fallen from the sky. Thus when Paul preached that 'gods made by hands are not gods at all' (Acts 19:26) this was not questioning the origin of their goddess and that for any complaints and disputes the courts were available. He also pointed out that the real danger was not the loss of trade but rather 'being charged with rioting', for which the Roman authorities might punish the city.

Paul wished to go among the crowd to defend himself, but was prevented from doing so by the disciples and 'some of the Asiarchs also, who were friends of his'.

Asiarchs were provincial officials responsible for the politico-religious organization of Asia in the worship of the goddess Roma and the emperors. They were in charge of the festivals and games, and while they were priests from a religious point of view, they were also officers of the imperial service. One of the titles of the reigning Asiarch was 'High Priest of Asia'. The reference in Acts to the representatives of the offical Roman cult as friends of Paul is an important point. Acts does not inform us about the apostle's imprisonment by the Roman authorities and his sufferings. On the contrary it tries to give the impression that Paul and the other early Christians moved within the confines of Roman law as they preached a 'licit religion', and were protected by it. Just as the town clerk's speech sounds like defending the Christian message, so also is the reference to the Asiarchs as friends of the apostle. Thus, Paul's troubles were just the result of popular hostility frequently incited by the local jews against which he was protected by friendly Roman officials.

It was soon after the riot that Paul left the city, probably following the advice of the Asiarchs. Acts does not inform us about Paul's route to Macedonia. His second letter to the Corinthians (2 Cor 2:12) mentions his going to Alexandria Troas first. His words give the impression that he may have not been able to preach here when he stopped during his second journey and now wanted to make it up. For this short trip if he did not take a boat but traversed the country, cities like Smyrna, Sardis and Pergamum, all with Jewish communities, stood on his way and he would have visited them.

In Alexandria Troas Paul waited for a while for Titus to join him here. The latter had been sent to Corinth previously with the so-called 'severe-letter'. When he did not show up Paul sailed to Neapolis and continued to Philippi. Paul's Greece and Macedonia sojourn took three months. Acts informs us that just as the apostle was about to leave directly for Antioch on the Orontes by ship the Jews in Greece had prepared an ambush against him (Acts 20:3). While some of Paul's party sailed to Alexandria Troas from here, Paul and Luke changed their minds and decided to travel overland to Macedonia which perhaps seemed safer. After arriving at Philippi the apostle and his friend took a boat from Neapolis to Alexandria Troas and met their friends. Altogether they stayed here for a week.

(opposite) Remains of the Roman road and the bridge which was once over the Tuzla çayı, river Satnioeis of the *Iliad*, by which Paul must have walked from Alexandria Troas to Assos.

'We sailed from Philippi after the feast of Unleavened Bread, and rejoined them five days later in Troas, where we spent a week' (Acts 20:6).

On the Saturday evening Paul, his friends and some other Christians met in one of the houses in Alexandria Troas 'to break bread,'[2] a term probably meant a fellowship meal in anticipation of Jesus' return rather than the type recalling the Last Supper. The place they met was probably a building of three storeys with rooms encircling a central inner courtyard. Here after the dinner, Paul began a very long lecture and 'talked on and on'; and the young Eutychus who was listening seated on a window sill of the third floor fell all the way down, on the floor of the room. He had fallen asleep, probably not only because of the long lecture but also the wine he may have had or the stuffy air caused by the resin torches or lamps in the room. Everybody thought that Eutychus was dead; but Paul throwing himself on the young boy's body told the others that there was nothing to worry about and the boy was fine. After his medical miracle Paul continued his talk which lasted until morning.

During this part of the journey the apostle and his friends were separated for a short while. While his friends took a boat Paul walked to Assos. The reason is not known. The apostle's companions may have decided that the hand of the plotting Jews in Greece might have reached here and they did not want to put Paul on a ship they did not know. Or Paul may have wanted to be by himself for a while to clear his mind. The idea of taking his ministry to Rome, his final goal, heart of the Gentile world, had been on his mind for a long time, and he was perhaps trying to make up his mind. He walked to Assos, the closest city with a harbour and met his friends there. During this long walk it would have been impossible to miss the sight of the Hellenistic temple of Apollo Smitheon[3] which was situated by the road some 15 km from Alexandria Troas. The temple housed a statue of Apollo crushing a mouse with his foot, made by the sculpter Scopas (active 370-330 BCE).

Set on a steep sloping hill, with spectacular views across the bay to Lesbos, Assos (Behramköy) was a beautiful and ancient city. It was now long past its

(opposite) Fishing port of Assos from which Paul sailed to Miletus and Palestine at the end of his third journey. Across the Aegean is Lesbos (Mitylene).

[2] The term used in Acts to show that from the very beginning Christians has special rites which distinguished them from Jews; the two types of meals were later converged.

[3] At the beginning of the *Iliad,* Apollo, who was worshipped in the region as 'Smitheon' or 'Mouse God' sends a pest to the lines of the Achaeans, which he does not stop until he is appeased.

great days, when in the fourth century BCE, the eunuch Hermeias, a former student of Plato, ruled here and whose friend Aristotle lived here for three years and married Pythia, the ruler's niece. Most of the ruins which have reached the present belong to the city which stood here at the time of Paul's visit. After walking for about 40 km from Alexandria Troas to Assos, Paul had, probably, neither the energy nor interest for a sightseeing tour of the city. Upon arrival he probably did not go up the acropolis but walked down to the small harbour, which is still in use today, and boarded the small coaster his companions had taken. The temple of Athena, which had stood on top of the hill since the sixth century BCE, would have been visible to him completely only after his vessel sailed some distance away from the harbour.

Thus the apostle got on the boat and all together with his friends carrying the money collected as gift for their brethren in Jerusalem they sailed from Assos to south making stops at the islands of Mitylene (Lesbos), Chios and Samos. After spending a night on Samos, Paul and his friends crossed to Anatolia and made another stop before Miletus at a point named Trogyllium, mentioned only in the Authorized Version (Acts 20:15). It is thought to have been situated on the southern shore of the cape formed by Mt Mycale (Samsun Dağı) whose tip is very close to Samos. Later visitors have named a small bay on this coast 'St Paul's anchorage.'

When Paul's coaster sailed into the harbour of Miletus the city stood on a promontory. Today, its remains lie some distance from the sea, thanks to the activity of the Meander river, moving and depositing silt which was already becoming a major problem then.[4] The river was then on the opposite side of the gulf, but now partly encircles the site in a large loop round the north. The best example of the silting up process is the gentle mound beyond the city, once the island of Lade, off which, in 494 BCE, 80 Milesian ships fought in vain against the Persians during the Ionian revolt.

The origin of the Christian congregation in Miletus is not known. While Paul may have visited the city during his long Ephesus stay and proclaimed the gospel, the Milesians may have also attended his preaching in Ephesus and been converted. The existence of a Jewish congregation in the city and

(opposite) Lion harbour of Miletus. Remains of the harbour monument. First century BCE. One of the tritons which decorated it has partly survived.

---

[4] The Anatolian coastline has receded about 10 km since Paul's time.

their interest in public spectacles is also attested to by an inscription on one of the steps of the large theatre, which in Greek reads 'Place for Jews who were also god-fearers'. The last word *theosebeis* which may also be translated as 'worshipers of God' is, in addition to Acts, used in ancient literature and encountered in inscriptions after the third century CE. The expression is thought to refer to Gentiles with a sort of attachment to the local Jewish community, although the extent of their association is not known and its meaning is thought to have varied from one place to the other. Nevertheless, it is known that the word referred to other people than proselytes who were circumcised. The Miletus inscription is thought to refer to either the local Jews themselves who may have used the term allegorically, or to proselytes who had become Jews, *Ioudaioi*, after having been circumcised and retained their previous definition. Although excavations have brought to light the traces of a building which is claimed to have been of a synagogue by the harbour it is not known if its history went back to Paul's time.

A stop in Ephesus may have caused new problems for Paul and his friends. He may have wished to avoid the risk of meeting his enemies. Nevertheless, it is not known if the Jewish community in Miletus fared better than that of Ephesus. From Miletus Paul sent to Ephesus and called to him the elders of the church. It is not known where Paul summoned the Ephesian elders. This is regarded one of the most touching episodes in the Acts of the apostles. He reminded his listeners of the opposition of the Jews in Ephesus which had caused him tears, trials, and imprisonment. That Paul made such a brief visit to a place with a large Jewish community, with the express purpose of seeing the elders from Ephesus and presumably other Asian centres, suggests that by now he no longer took the gospel to the Jews, or at least, not here. Now he was on his way to Jerusalem expecting more affliction, which he saw as a culmination of his ministry. He was deeply concerned about heretics and schismatics in Ephesus, and he admonished the elders to remain alert, commending them to God. The elders wept that they would not see the apostle again. Acts does not inform us about the length of the apostle's stay here but it was probably not longer than a few days. After he decided that his mission here was over, putting the church in their care he walked to the harbour of farewell and embarked on a ship and continued his return voyage to Caesarea.

(opposite) Inscription in the fifth row of spectators' seats from the theatre at Miletus. Late Roman period. In Greek it reads: 'Place for Jews who were also god-fearers'.

"But now I know that none of you to whom I preached the kingdom during my travels will ever see my face again" (Acts 20:25).

The Anatolian part of Paul's return trip which began at Assos came to an end at the Lycian port of Patara. Until here the apostle probably used one or more small coasters which sailed for short laps from one Greek island or port to the other carrying any kind of available passenger or merchandise along the coast of Anatolia. At Patara the apostle and his companions had to find another vessel, obviously a larger one which could sail the high seas, bound to Tyre on the Phoenician coast (Acts 21:1-2).

Patara on the south west Lycian coast was one of the principal cities of the region. Its original Lycian name was 'Pttara', later mistakenly thought to have derived from the Latin *patera*, a sort of cup. It obviously owed its existence to a narrow but long natural harbour at the mouth of the river Xanthus (Eşen çayı) which is now flowing on the northwest of the ruins. The city was also famous for its oracle of Apollo, where it was believed, the god spent the winter, having been in Delos for the summer. Apollo was the most popular god in Lycia where he was worshipped as 'Lykeios', 'Wolf God' and had given the region its name.[5] Most of what is visible at the site today had not been constructed when Paul changed ships here and dates mainly from the late first and more so, the second centuries. The only visible construction that Paul might have seen on his very brief visit, was a small theatre which lay on a hillside to the south east, at the same spot as the present day one half hidden by dunes and the forerunner of the colossal lighthouse which helped pilots to locate the entrance of the harbour at night situated on the same hill.

Sometime after Paul stopped here Patara became one of the Roman grain supply stations and in the reign of Hadrian (117-38), who is known to have visited the city, a large granary was built on the western side of the quay. The giant rock-cut cistern situated on top of the mountain above the theatre whose history must have dated to the pre-Pauline period is clear evidence of the scarcity of the sweet water supply in this dry and hot region. The miracles of St Nicholas, who was born in Patara and would later become famous as the bishop of Myra in the fourth century, which are related to the discovery and purification of wells, were not incidental and show the value that the local people afforded to water.

(opposite) Remains of the theatre and other ruins at Patara looking north.

'Paul had decided to sail past Ephesus in order not to lose time in the province of Asia, for he was hurrying to be in Jerusalem, if at all possible, for the day of Pentecost' (Acts 20:16).

[5] Greek *Lykos*, 'wolf'.

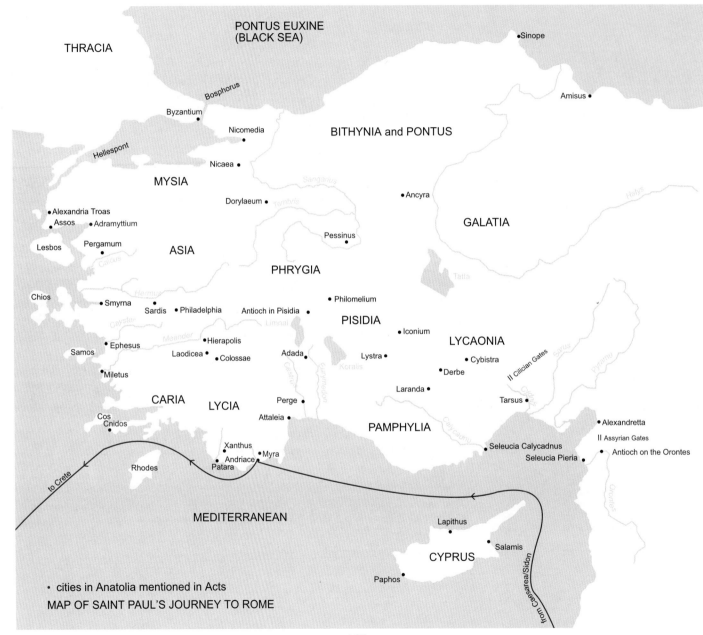

THRACIA

PONTUS EUXINE
(BLACK SEA)

•Sinope

Amisus•

Bosphorus

Byzantium•

BITHYNIA and PONTUS

Hellespont

Nicomedia•

MYSIA

Nicaea•

Sangarius

•Ancyra

Dorylaeum•

Tembris

GALATIA

•Alexandria Troas
Assos• •Adramyttium

Pessinus•

Lesbos   Pergamum•

ASIA

Halys

Caicus

PHRYGIA

Chios

Hermus

•Philomelium

•Smyrna

Sardis• •Philadelphia

Antioch in Pisidia•

PISIDIA

•Iconium

Cayster

Limnai

LYCAONIA

Samos   •Ephesus

Meander

•Hierapolis

Laodicea• •Colossae

Adada
•

Lystra•

•Cybistra

II Cilician Gates

Sarus

Pyramu

•Miletus

Castro

Eurymedon

Koralis

•Derbe

Laranda•

Tarsus•

CARIA   LYCIA

•Perge

Attaleia•

PAMPHYLIA

Calycadnu

•Alexandretta

II Assyrian Gates

Cos
Cnidos

Xanthus
•
Andriace •Myra

Seleucia Calycadnus•

• Antioch on the Orontes
Seleucia Pieria

to Crete

Rhodes   Patara

Orontes

MEDITERRANEAN

•Lapithus

from Caesarea/Sidon

CYPRUS

•Salamis

•Paphos

• cities in Anatolia mentioned in Acts

MAP OF SAINT PAUL'S JOURNEY TO ROME

PAUL'S JOURNEY TO ROME

Caesarea — Sidon — **Myra — Cnidus** — Lasea — Malta — Syracuse —
Rhegium — Puteoli — Forum of Appius — Three Taverns — Rome

In the autumn of 60, Paul and a group of other prisoners, unlike Paul who were not citizens 'on appeal', were put on a short-haul coaster of Syrian registration at Caesarea. Paul was accompanied by Aristarchus, 'a Macedonian from Thessalonica' and Luke himself. The destination of the vessel was perhaps Adramyttium (Edremit) where it had come from, a small prosperous coastal city on the Aegean coast of Anatolia opposite Lesbos.

It was probably late October, the end of the navigation period for the high seas and the centurion Julius from Cohort Augusta, who was in charge of the prisoners, was unable to find a vessel which would have taken them directly to one of the ports of Italy. Luke might have included Cohort Augusta, the name of the Roman legion based in Syria during this period, to increase the prominence of the prisoner Paul. The frequent appearance of centurions in Acts (10:1, 21:32, 23:17, 24:23, 27:1) gives Paul's story a military atmosphere like the crucifixion of Jesus, at which there was a centurion standing. The season was late and the centurion might have even regarded himself lucky in finding a vessel 'bound for ports in the province of Asia'. From there, he would have crossed the Aegean by another vessel as Paul had done several times during his missionary journeys and after Philippi continued overland by way of the Via Egnatia[1] until the Adriatic. The latter was another military artery that the Romans had built and it connected Byzantium to Dyrrachium. Across the channel another thoroughfare, the Via Appia, began at Brindisium and ran until Rome.

After a brief stop at Sidon, where Paul was allowed by his custodian 'to visit his friends who took care of him' the vessel set sail, its captain making use of the currents which run to the northern along the coastline of Syria and Anatolia and round the lee of Cyprus 'because of the headwinds, and acrossing the open sea off the coast of Cilicia and Pamphylia' (Acts 27:2-5). Thus, passing Cyprus by its northern coast and after leaving Cape Gelidonya behind, they made a stop in Myra before continuing on towards the Hellespont. At the time that Paul's vessel sailed into Andriace, Myra's port, the region

'We went on board a ship from Adramyttium bound for ports in the province of Asia and set sail' (Acts 27:2).

[1] Some fifty years later Ignatius of Antioch, as a Roman prisoner, would be escorted from Alexandria Troas to Macedonia by the same way for his long trip to Rome to be martyred there during the reign of Trajan (98-117).

after going through the Persian and later the Ptolemaic hegemonies had been in 43 annexed to the Roman empire by Claudius. Although this mountainous region did not have any other natural resource than its timber, owing to its location on the major routes of the maritime trade it was in close contact with the rest of the world. The existence of Jewish communities in the region is attested to by the information in the First Book of Maccabees (15:23-24). According to this, among the cities to which the Roman consul sent letters in the middle of the second century BCE to inform them about the imperial protection granted to the Jews, Myndos, Caria, Lycia, Halicarnassus, Cnidus, Side and Phaselis are mentioned.

Short stays in the ports of Lycia was not something particular just for the vessel which was carrying Paul. Since antiquity it had become a custom for the maritime traffic coming from the Mediterranean to shelter at one of the well-protected Lycian ports and wait for favourable winds. These ports offered shelter to a crowded sea traffic leaving for all directions, the Aegean, the Mediterranean or the Black Sea throughout the navigation season and also gave captains a chance to do some extra business on the way.

Myra, situated by the Myros (Demre) river, was an important city of Lycia in the Classical and Hellenistic era. Its name is thought to come from the Greek word for myrrh. Strabo describes the city being on a high crest, that is the precipitous hill which now rises behind the theatre. The inhabited city was on the level ground at the foot of the hill. Although isolated from the interior by the mountains rising up to 3,000 m, the Lycian coastal cities were in close contact with the rest of the world through their maritime contacts. In the apocrypal Acts of Paul, the apostle came to Myra where he cured several locals. Later Thecla rejoined him here.

The city's harbour was at Andriace at the mouth of the river Andracus a few kilometres away. Andriace, like Patara, was an important port under the Romans for supplying grain to the troops campaigning in the east, and the granary which was dedicated to Trajan and Hadrian is the largest of its kind in Anatolia. The cistern built below the courtyard of the market-place is probably the largest in Anatolia and gives an idea of the large number of vessels to which it must have supplied sweet water.

Even though the season was late at the time that the vessel carrying Paul sailed into the bay of Andriace there must have been numerous vessels anchored along the dock some probably prepared to spend the winter here. Among these ships the custodian of the prisoners came across a freight vessel carrying corn to Italy. This was probably one of the fleet which regularly carried grain from Egypt to Italy. Such large vessels

(opposite) A Roman sarcophagus in Andriace, the silted port of Myra looking south. In the background are the ruins of the buildings which were lined along the wharf.

had to sail upwind and frequently when chased by contrary winds sheltered in Lycian harbours. The season was late for such large merchant ships and this was a coincidence. The vessel he found was probably one of those which regularly carried grain between Egypt and Italy and the captain during its already late last voyage stopped at Myra perhaps with the hope of finding some passengers. Suetonius informs us that Claudius 'employed to ship grain [to Rome] even in the winter season. For he guaranteed the merchant shippers profits by assuming himself any losses someone might suffer on account of storms, and he instituted great rewards for those who built merchant ships.' The half-walnut-shell shape of a usual grain-freighter made it known in Greek as *gaulos* or bathtub. It usually bore a single sail carried on a single mast and had to be towed in and out of harbour. The cost of sea transportation for merchandise was about one fifth of the cost by land and Egypt was the most important grain source for Rome. During this period Claudius had given special privileges to shipowners who could carry a minimum of 70 tons of wheat. To sail the high seas these grain freighters were the best because in addition to offering room and safety they did not make calls at many ports. However, since they were built for carrying cargo the facilities were limited. Apart from a few cabins used by the skipper or important passengers such as the owner of the cargo or his agent there was no room but the deck. The ship's supply consisted only of water. The travellers had to have their own food, bedding, wine etc.

The centurion probably bore a *diplomum,* a pass which gave him priority to use any facility he required with or without payment until he took his prisoners to Rome. Before sailing the Ionian sea Paul's ship tried to make a stop at Cnidos in Caria. Although devoid of arable land and sufficient water the rocky promontory on which Cnidus was founded enjoyed two small harbours which offered shelter to sea traffic, especially to those which arrived from the south and had to wait for the northwestern gale to stop before continuing on their way. The commercial activities that they carried out with the vessels which sailed in and out of their ports were the major income of the Cnidians. The ship carrying Paul being unable to shelter to Cnidus because of the inclement weather and continued its way to find a better harbour.

The 'We-sections' in Acts come to an end with the arrival of Paul and his companions in Rome. Acts does not make it clear if the latter stayed in Rome while Paul was under house arrest which ultimately ended with his martyrdom in about the year 62. Luke, the author of Acts may have also martyred during the persecutions by Nero.

Later sources and Paul's Pastoral Letters inform us that Paul was tried and acquitted and made another journey to Spain, Anatolia (Ephesus and Alexandria Troas), Crete and Macedonia before he was arrested taken to Rome to be martyred there.

(opposite) Detail from a manuscript showing the martyrdoms of Peter and Paul. 1170. The British Museum.

"For I am already being poured out like a libation, and the time of my departure is at hand" (2 Tim 4:6).

S·PAVLVS

S·PETR·

OR·S·VBIO·QVA·DRIGAS

NOS·DVCAT·AD·PATRIA·CIS

THE STORY OF THECLA

The story of Thecla, the most famous virgin martyr of early Christianity, is narrated in the apocryphal Acts of Paul which is thought to have been recorded towards the end of the second century in Anatolia. Its popularity has led some scholars to believe that the story may have been based on a real Christian martyr of the same name.

If it may be summarized very briefly, for Paul celibacy was an ideal Christian condition because it did not prescribe any worldly obligation which might prevent him from devotion to the Lord. This message and the absurdity of marriage in the light of the expected Kingdom of God was taken further in the course of time and became a source of popularity of legends of virgins in Anatolia.

The legend of Thecla begins with Paul's flight from Antioch in Pisidia to Iconium and his preaching there. His praise of the 'virgin life' and its rewards attracted a certain girl of eighteen years, named Thecla, who sat and listened to Paul at the open window of her house, because her mother did not let her go and listen to the apostle. Thecla's mother, alarmed about the devotion of her daughter to the preaching of Paul, took the news to the girl's fiancé Thamyris, saying 'for three days and three nights Thecla did not arise from the window, neither to eat nor to drink...this man upset the whole city of the Iconians...for all the women and the young men go in to him'. When Thamyris' efforts to prevent the young girl from listening to the apostle gave no result, together with other men of Iconium he brought the problem to the governor and Paul was arrested and thrown into prison for corrupting the maidens of their city, teaching them to stay virgins and not to marry, thus disregarding the traditional customs.

When Thecla learned what had happened, she left her home in secret and bribing her way past the guards with her jewellery, entered the prison and

Icon of St Thecla. Twentieth century. St Barnabas Museum. North Cyprus.

'went in to Paul and sat by his feet and heard the wonderful works of God...as she kissed his chains'.

The following morning, however, when she was found in the prison, the governor ordered Paul to be beaten and thrown out of the city. Thecla was condemned to be burned in the theatre so that this might teach a lesson to 'all the woman which have been taught' by the apostle. When the pile of wood on which she was placed was lighted, a sudden rainshower began and put out the pyre and Thecla escaped. She found Paul in a new tomb outside the city where he was hiding and together the two went to Antioch.[1] Thecla told Paul that she would cut off her hair and dress as a man and follow him. Paul, however, did not take her seriously and refused to baptize her.

In Antioch a Syrian nobleman named Alexander saw Thecla and tried to buy her from Paul with money and gifts. But the apostle responded 'I know not the woman of whom you speak, neither she is mine'. When the man tried to rape her, she resisted and tearing the man's cloak and taking his crown with the figure of Caesar from his head made him a laughing-stock in the city.

Thecla, taken before the governor, was charged with sacrilege and condemned to the beasts. Several attempts to carry out the verdict failed. She was thrown naked to a fierce lioness, but the animal merely licked her feet. For a second time she was stripped and thrown into the arena, and wild animals were let loose upon her. The lioness killed the other animals but she was also slain. This time Thecla jumped into the great tank of water which appeared upon her prayer saying 'In the name of Jesus Christ do I baptize myself on the last day'. A cloud enveloped her so that her nakedness could not be seen. When the last beast let into the theatre did not touch her she was bound by the feet between the bulls and hot irons were put under the animals' bellies, but the flame burned the ropes and she was saved. Meanwhile a

[1] The texts say only 'Antioch' and which one is disputed.

queen Tryphaena who had lost her daughter a short while ago and who had given Thecla shelter in her house was among the spectators. When she fainted the governor thought that she had died and worrying that the emperor might punish the city, stopped the games. Thecla was forgiven. Queen Tryphaena is a historical personage, who was the widow of king Cotys of Thrace and the mother of Polemo II, the last king of Pontus, also a great-niece of the emperor Claudius, it is not known how she was incorporated in the story.

The romance ends with Thecla having dressed herself as a boy in search of Paul whom she found at Myra in Lycia. Here Paul healed Hermocrates of dropsy and restored sight to Hermippus, the older son of Hermocrates. Thecla told the apostle her sufferings for Christ's sake and received her baptism: 'I have received the washing, O Paul; for he that has worked together with thee in the Gospel has worked with me also unto my baptizing'. Later, Thecla returned to Iconium but did not stay there. From there she went to Seleucia on Calycadnus (Silifke) where she retired to a cave on Mt Calamon and lived to the age of ninety. When she was threatened by men, who were jealous of her healing powers, for she was by then running a nunnery which threatened the business of local healers, she was saved by the rock of her cave opening to receive her. Although she died peacefully in her cave she was regarded as the first Christian woman martyr. Her sanctuary became a popular place of pilgrimage. A tradition adds that she went underground to Rome which accounts for the presence of her body there.

Christian tradition regards a cave at Silifke's 'Meryemlik' district as the place where Thecla disappeared into the rock. In the fourth century the cave was probably enlarged and given the shape of an underground basilica. The reused building material shows that there was probably a Roman building here, and the site may originally have been a pagan shrine. Pilgrimage to the cave church was revered throughout Byzantine history and at one time its walls were probably decorated with mosaics. During the second half of the fifth century a large church, the largest one ever built in Cilicia, was built over the cave.Only a section of its apse has survived to the present.

Remains of the apse (westernmost quarter) of the church built above the grotto of St Thecla.

PAUL'S LETTERS

Apart from Acts, the letters of Paul to the churches he had founded or with which he was familiar are the other main source for our knowledge of his apostolic work and of course, for the apostle himself. These letters also make up for the compressed text of Acts and thus help us to understand what is missing about his journeys. Written to his followers at virtually the same time as events with which they deal, they are the earliest works of the New Testament.

Paul's surviving writings constitute a small corpus of nine letters addressed to particular churches, one private letter, and three letters to Timothy and Titus, known as the 'pastoral letters'. Three of these letters were written to communities in Anatolia: Galatians, Colossians and Ephesians; whilst scholarly opinion is divided as to whether the latter two are genuine, Galatians is indisputably so. Acts and the letters seem to be independent of each other, even though the letters were in existence when Acts was written.

Paul seems to have regarded himself as responsible, in addition to the churches he established, for 'all the churches' he knew (2 Cor 11:28) and corresponded with them. He may have also visited most of them once or more. This was a period during which, except for the military postal service, people had to rely on other people going in the direction of their letters to correspond with others. In the lively social and commercial world of the first century which was made possible by the Roman peace there seems to have been no shortage of such people. Paul wrote (dictated) his letters in *Koine* or common language, the Hellenistic Greek of his day. This was the *lingua franca*, the international language needed by any man in public life or one travelling or writing, spread by the armies of Alexander and the Hellenistic kingdoms which succeeded his empire. However, Paul's Greek was not as distinguished as that of Luke, the author of Acts and in accordance with the practice of the time his letters were composed by professional scribes.

Paul's words that there was 'a letter allegedly from us' (2 Thes 2:2) in circulation show that even then his letters were forged. This is the reason that as he mentioned (2 Thes 3:17) he signed his letters by his 'own hand'. His drawing attention to the extra large script (Gal 6:11) to show the authenticity of his letter, was mistakenly interpreted as his having bad eyesight.

Letter to the Galatians

This letter is also regarded as one of the earliest documents of the Christian church. Shortly after his return to Antioch on the Orontes, probably visitors from Galatia informed Paul that Jewish Christians known as Judaizers were preaching a narrow type of Christianity among the small congregations that the apostle had established during his missionary activity, and that some of his Galatian converts had turned away from his teaching. These Judaizers insisted that the converts should be circumcised and follow the other requirements of the Mosaic law.

Paul may have heard the news of Galatia at the time he was being opposed by similar Jews in Judea on the issue of circumcision and Jews' dietary laws. Instead of visiting them he wrote to 'the churches of Galatia'[1] (Gal 1:2), meaning the Christian congregations in Antioch in Pisidia, Iconium, Lystra, and Derbe, a circular letter which is regarded as one of the most remarkable documents in the New Testament. At its beginning the apostle expresses his surprise when he says 'I am amazed that you are so quickly forsaking, the one who called you by [the] grace [of Christ] for a different gospel' (Gal 1:6). How could his first converts whom he had seen and preached to less than a year before have done this? They were his first children and he could not let them err.

On his first visit, he wrote, they had received him 'as an angel of God, as Christ Jesus' (Gal 4:14). They would have plucked out their own eyes to give him (Gal 4:15). Although his expression 'stupid Galatians' or 'Are you so stupid' is not a usual manner of address, this he said to compare them with the Celtic people of the region, who were well-known for their simple-mindedness in antiquity and to accuse them of acting like these natives. Now, they had turned from the liberty of the gospel to the old bondage of custom and tradition. Paul said to the Galatians 'I would like to be with you now and to change my tone, for I am perplexed because of you' (Gal 4:20). Dictated in a hurry, the letter was written by one of the many scribes who existed in every major town,

---

[1] Most of the scholars agree that the apostle could not have meant Galatia proper where he had not been, and as he referred to the Christians in Thessalonica or Philippi as 'Macedonians', here he referred to the Christians in southern part of the province as 'Galatians'.

and signed by the apostle with large letters at the end (Gal 6:11). The absence of any remark about the abrogation of the obligation of circumcision for Gentile converts, a matter concerning the Galatians, shows that it may have been written before the Apostolic Council in Jerusalem.

It has also been suggested that Paul may have thought that the decisions waiving the most important of the obligations of the Mosaic law in the Apostolic Council in Jerusalem would not carry much weight among such rural congregations and that he had not mentioned it. If this hypotheses is supplemented by the fact that the interpretation of the Greek word *proteron* (Gal 4:13) not as 'originally' but 'formerly' or 'on the first of two occasions' it may be concluded that the letter would have been written after the second journey; during the long Ephesus stay of the third journey, when he is known to have written most of his letters.

First letter to the Corinthians

Paul had founded the church at Corinth during his second missionary journey. His epistle known as the first letter to the Corinthians is an example of the excited correspondence which took place between the apostle and the churches he had founded.

Paul says he had written a letter to the Corinthians asking them not to associate themselves with immoral people (1 Cor 5:9). Some parts of this letter are thought to have also survived incorporated in his second letter to the Corinthians.

Not much later three members of the Corinthian congregation, Stephanas, Achaicus, and Fortunatus had come to him in Ephesus (1 Cor 16:17) with another letter asking about such matters as the relationship between the sexes, the meaning of marriage, engagement, and divorce. Another question of deep concern dealt with the purchase of meat from animals sacrificed at pagan shrines. They also wondered if the purchase of such meat necessarily meant the support of pagan cults. They wondered how people were to conduct themselves in church and if women should cover their heads in church. They also wanted the advice of the apostle about the practice of speaking in tongues, an early Christian term which refers to ecstatic speech. The Corinthians seem to have answered the apostle by asking more of his advice; on subjects such as sex, marriage or circumcision to which he replied at length in 1 Cor 7.

Shortly after this, Paul received some visitors from Corinth. In his letter the apostle refers to them as 'Chloe's people'. They may have been her slaves, freedmen, or employees. The news they brought to him was disturbing. The Christians at the church of Corinth which he had founded during his second missionary journey were breaking up into factions about their favourite teachers by whom they had been converted and about the type of Christianity they may have been taught; one Apollos, the eloquent Alexandrian Jewish convert, or Kephas (Peter) who must have preached there at some time and others. Even more serious were the incidents of immoral conduct reported by the messengers. The Corinthian Christians had turned to pagan courts for the settlement of their business disagreements and, far more serious yet, their celebration of the Lord's Supper had become a drinking bout.

Paul replied to all of these issues in detail in a letter. In his closing remarks of this letter he mentioned his desire to visit Corinth, and he shared with them his plans to visit Macedonia, but at the same time he said 'I shall stay in Ephesus until Pentecost, because a door has opened to me wide, and productive for work, but there are many opponents' (1 Cor 16:8-9) referring, perhaps, to the approaching festival of Artemis during which he might have a chance to preach to the strangers who would flock to Ephesus.

Second letter to the Corinthians

Neither Paul's letter to the Corinthians, nor his sending Timothy (Acts 19:22, by way of Macedonia) restored the peace within the church there. Certain Jewish Christians carrying letters of recommendation had shown up in Corinth (2 Cor 3:1) and were claiming the right to exercise authoritative leadership in the church. Paul had to interrupt his Ephesus stay to sail directly from Ephesus to Cenchreae, the eastern port of Corinth. For Paul this was a very distressing visit. Failing to achieve his objective, he returned to Ephesus, his authority badly shaken. He could not accept defeat but he did not want to make 'another painful' visit (2 Cor 2:1) and his only alternative was to address another letter to the Corinthian Christians, known as the second letter to the Corinthians, or the 'severe letter' in which he argued, plead and threatened. Titus took the letter across the Aegean. It was again Titus who delivered the good news of the Corinthian church's repentance when he was in Macedonia. Paul, now happy about the development of events wrote a third letter to the Corinthians incorporated in the second letter.

Letter to the Ephesians

The fact that this document does not contain any detailed information about either the Ephesians, with whom Paul had spent about three years or about any other Christian congregation with whom he was familiar, has led some scholars to believe that it is a circular letter to be read to the members of any congregation whose name could have replaced that of 'in Ephesus' at its beginning: 'Paul, an apostle of Christ Jesus by the will of God, to the holy ones who are [in Ephesus] faithful in Christ Jesus' (Eph 1:1). If it had been written to the Ephesians with whom the apostle had spent three years it would have made more than the single reference, which is to Tychicus (Eph 6:21). Also if it was written in Ephesus, it is odd that he should write a letter to Ephesians from Ephesus. The grammatical analysis of the text also implies another hand. It may even have been written after the martyrdom of the apostle by one of his disciples.

Paul's words that he was 'a prisoner for the Lord' (Eph 4:1) leads one to think that in addition to the probalitiy of Ephesus, he was either in Caesarea where he was also imprisoned (Acts 24:23) or Rome under house arrest while he was waiting for his appeal.

A section which survives in Paul's letter to the Romans, (Rom 16:1-24) is, however, thought to have been a part of a letter to the Ephesians. This letter was dictated by the apostle during his three-month sojourn in Corinth and is regarded as his oldest letter after the one he wrote to the Galatians.

Phoebe, a deaconess of the church of Cenchreae, was about to go to Ephesus and the apostle did not miss the chance to introduce her to his fellow Christians in Ephesus and send them his greeting.

Paul's message to the Ephesians sheds interesting light upon the Christian community in Ephesus.[1] The apostle begins sending his greetings to Priscilla (Prisca) and Aquila, who had already 'risked their necks' for him. Their house was also being used as a church (Rom 16:3-4). A special greeting is extended

[1] It is also claimed that all the names included in this letter may have belonged to Roman Christians some of whom Paul met, some he knew by name.

113

to the 'beloved Epaenetus, who was the first fruits in Asia for Christ' (Rom 16:5). Andronicus and Junia, who had been fellow prisoners with Paul are referred to as 'relatives' and 'prominent among the apostles' (Rom 16:7). They had accepted the Christian faith before Paul, and perhaps had been converted by John. Ampliatus is the apostle's 'beloved in the Lord' (Rom 16:8) and Urbanus is his 'co-worker in Christ' (Rom 16:9). Then there is his 'beloved Stachys' (Rom 16:9), who may be the leader of the house church in Hierapolis, where Philip proclaimed the gospel. It is not known if Aristobulus, to whose family greetings are sent, was the Aristobulus who was said to be the brother of Barnabas. This was a common name then and it may have referred to another person. Greetings are also sent to 'Asyncritus, Phlegon, Hermes, Patrobas, Hermas and the brothers who are with them' (Rom 16:14) and to 'Philolagus, Julia, Nereus and his sister, and Olympas, and all the holy ones who are with them' (Rom 16:15). A special greeting is extended to 'Rufus, chosen in the Lord, and his mother and mine' (Rom 16:13). The long list of names indicates a closeness with a Christian community which Paul may have gained during a long and intense ministry such as in Ephesus.

Letter to the Philippians

The fact that Polycarp referred to the 'letters' that Paul had written to the Philippians imply that in the early church there was more than a single letter that the apostle had written to them, and the surviving single letter, probably include excerpts from his other letters.

It seems that when the church in Philippi heard that the apostle was in prison, where obviously he was able to receive visitors, they raised money and sent by Epaphroditus, to stay with him. Unfortunately, Epaphroditus fell dangerously ill while waiting on Paul, and when he recovered he returned to Philippi. Thereupon, Paul sent a letter, to protect Epaphroditus from being criticized for leaving while he was still in prison.

In his letter the apostle answers the questions of the Philippians, which Epaphroditus probably told him, and informs the Philippians he seemed to be convinced that he would be acquitted (Phil 1:24), yet in spite of this hope and conviction, he still considered the possibility of condemnation (Phil 2:17). The references to the 'praetorium', or the 'palace' (Phil 1:13) and 'those of Caesar's household' (Phil 4:22) indicate that he had come to know some people stationed in a palace which was put to use for the Roman governor. These references may have also pointed to Caesarea or Rome as the place of origin of the letter. Since in Rome he lived in his own hired house, Caesarea seems to be a better candidate. On stylistic grounds scholars prefer an earlier date than that of the above events. Although Acts is silent about it the apostle may have been imprisoned in Ephesus from where he wrote it. In some of the Roman provinces, in addition to the Roman governor who was a proconsul, there was a procurator who was in charge of handling the finances of all kinds, his term being longer than that of one-year term of the governor. It was probably this second group of officials who required a large and permanent 'household' to whom Paul was referring. The term may refer to the procurator's relatives and servants (slaves or freedmen). He shared with them his convictions and some of them had accepted the Christian faith.

Letter to the Colossians

It is not known whether Paul ever visited Colossae, though clearly he took an interest in the church there, writing to them from prison. More probably it was Epaphras (Col 1:7) who took Christianity to the city and neighbouring Laodicea and Hierapolis. His words 'for those in Laodicea and all who have not seen me face to face' (Col 2:1) imply that although he may have passed through the region on his way to Ephesus during his third journey he may not have met many people there. Nevertheless, Colossians had probably heard about him.

As far as the origin of the letter is concerned, it has the same ambiguity as the letter to the Ephesians. Shortly after the arrival of the runaway slave Onesimus, Epaphras, the leader of the church in Colossae, came to where Paul was imprisoned: Ephesus, Caesarea or Rome, and informed the apostle of the situation in his parish. He reported that the Colossians were attracted by some more sophisticated cults than what was preached by the apostle. These consisted of various syncretic forms of their old philosophy and oriental beliefs and speculations. This new teaching both threatened the belief in Christ's supremacy and created an esoteric group of Christians claiming superiority over the average Christians. They thought that physical matter was tainted with sin and, therefore, the incarnate Christ was inferior to angels (Col 2:8).

Mound of Colossae looking west.

Paul answered the dissenting theologians in Colossae by exposing the heresy of their philosophy and stressing the adequacy of Christ: 'Think of what is above, not of what is on earth' (Col 3:2). To his advice to the Colossians, the apostle had added that masters must treat their slaves justly and fairly for they also had a master in heaven; he was sending the young Onesimus back to Colossae with Tychicus who took the letter.

Colossae was founded on two hills side by side by the river Lycus. By the first century CE the city was no longer the large and prosperous city it had been in the fifth century BCE, when the Persian king Xerxes stopped here on his way to the conquest of Greece, according to Herodotus. Some eighty years later, in 401 BCE, Cyrus the Younger travelled through the region in the opposite direction. The Seleucids, who did not miss the position of the city on the north-south and east-west military routes, had refounded it.

Beginning in the first century Colossae suffered several earthquakes and by the Byzantine era in around the eighth century the town had fallen into oblivion. Thus in the Middle Ages many people thought that the Colossians addressed by Paul in his letter were the inhabitants of the island of Rhodes, because of their famous Colossus, one of the seven wonders of the world.

Letter to Philemon

While Paul was still in prison, together with Timothy and Epaphras, Onesimus,[1] a young runaway slave from Colossae, came to the prison to see the apostle. He had perhaps stolen from his master when he left and he hoped Paul somehow could free him from slavery. He was won to the Christian faith by the apostle.

Paul realized his obligation to the slave's owners, Philemon, Apphia, and Archippus, prosperous Christians from Colossae. He would have liked to keep Onesimus 'so that he might serve me on your behalf in my imprisonment for the gospel' (Phlm 13), although for all concerned it was necessary to send Onesimus back to his masters.

Paul sent with Onesimus a letter addressed to the slave's masters, and the church that met in their house commending the slave to them as a trustworthy Christian, and appealing to Philemon to forgive Onesimus and to receive him as a beloved brother. Since Paul knew the punishments that a runaway slave would be subject to, he wrote with authority to align the moral sentiment of the whole church in his appeal to Philemon. From Paul's letter to the Colossians it is clear that Onesimus returned to his master in company with Tychicus (Col 4:7-9). It is obvious that the slave was not only received well but may even have been freed. Some of the personal references in the letter are similar to those in Paul's letter to the Colossians.

At the end of the letter by saying 'prepare a guest room for me' (Phlm 22) he shows his intention of visiting Colossae.

[1] He is often identified with the bishop of Ephesus, referred to by Ignatius in his letter to the Ephesians. 'Onesimus' was however, one of the common names of that period.

Abbreviations

Acts	Acts of the Apostles	Jn	John
BCE	Before the Common Era (BC)	1 Kgs	1 Kings
CE	Common Era (AD)	2 Kgs	2 Kings
1 Chr	1 Chronicles	Lk	Luke
2 Chr	2 Chronicles	1 Mc	1 Maccabees
Col	Colossians	Mk	Mark
1 Cor	1 Corinthians	Mt	Matthew
2 Cor	2 Corinthians	Phil	Philippians
Dt	Deuteronomy	p	page
Eph	Ephesians	Phlm	Philemon
Ez	Ezekiel	Rom	Romans
Gal	Galatians	St	Saint
Heb	Hebrews	2 Thes	2 Thessalonians
Is	Isiah	2 Tim	2 Timothy

In spelling ancient names of places and persons, their most popular forms in English have been used. The Turkish equivalent of names and the reign of rulers are usually mentioned in parentheses when it is thought this would help to understand the events better. All biblical quotations are from the New American Bible, 1987 edition, Nashville, USA. The dates which are not marked as BCE (BC) or Before the Common Era, are Common Era, CE (AD). The dates of rulers, as in Claudius (41-54), indicate their reigns.

(opposite) One of the hundreds of graffiti which Christians carved to consecrate pagan temples and tombs in Anatolia, especially after Christianity became a free religion in the fourth century. In Greek it reads: 'Jesus Christ, Nika (Victory)'. Arycanda. Lycia.

OTHER TITLES